The Guinness Book

Marriage

The Guinness Book of

Marriage

Valerie Porter

GUINNESS PUBLISHING

Project Editor: Honor Head
Assistant Editor: Paola Simoneschi
Design and Layout: Eric Drewery
Picture Editor: Alex Goldberg
Picture Credits: John Frost, Historical Newspaper Service
                Gamma
                The Hulton-Deutsch Collection
                National Gallery
                Popperfoto
                Rex Features Ltd.

Published in Great Britain by Guinness Publishing Ltd,
33 London Road, Enfield, Middlesex

Typeset in Goudy Old Style and Rockwell Light by
Ace Filmsetting Ltd, Frome, Somerset
Printed and bound in Great Britain by
The Bath Press, Bath, Avon

A catalogue record for this book is available from the British
Library.

ISBN 0-85112-943-9

Contents

Chapter 4
Now That We're Married

❝

*My definition of marriage: it resembles
a pair of shears, so joined that they
cannot be separated; often moving in
opposite directions, yet always
punishing anyone who comes between
them.*

Rev Sydney Smith, 1771–1845

❞

❝——————————————

When you're a married man, Samivel, you'll understand a good many things as you don't understand now; but vether it's worth while goin' through so much to learn so little, as the charity-boy said ven he got to the end of the alphabet, is a matter of taste.

Charles Dickens *Pickwick Papers*

——————————————**❞**

1
Anticipation

QUE SERA

"

When I grew up and fell in love,
I asked my sweetheart, 'What lies
  ahead?'
Here's what my sweetheart said:
'Que sera, sera; whatever will be, will
  be,
The future's not ours to see; que sera,
  sera.'

"

Seven out of ten people in Britain get married at some stage of their lives and, although four marriages in ten end in divorce, it seems that the great majority of young people want to get married – one day – and nearly all the rest want to find a partner, if not for life then at least to ease the basic incompleteness of the individual. Human beings, impatient with the present, seek to know the future and look for signs and auguries to predict *que sera*, and one of the major areas of interest to those wanting to know the future is the identity of the partner who will share it with them.

The best dates for such marriage divination are said to be the eves of certain festivals: **St Agnes** (21st January) or **St Martin** (25th April), for example, or **Hallowe'en** (31st October), **Christmas Eve** (24th December), or the eve of the **Celtic Summer** (30th April).

HALLOWE'EN

Traditionally, **Hallowe'en** has been a favourite time for divining the future, especially with regard to lovers and marriage partners. It is the eve of the Celtic winter, a season which until the early part of this century was the most popular time for marriages (for superstitious reasons). Apples, nuts and seeds are the most traditional media for such messages – they are all symbols of fertility anyway, and the trees that bear apples and nuts have long been associated with the 'other world', and have been regarded as magical or holy in many parts of the world. (Eve, incidentally, is said in *The Bible* to have eaten the 'fruit of the tree' – there is no specific mention of it being an apple.)

There are numerous divination rituals for Hallowe'en, some of them more fruity(!) than others . . . **Peel an apple** in one long strip and throw the peel over your left shoulder – it will lie on the ground in the shape of the initial of your future partner. In the pioneering days of America they even had peel-paring 'bees' (parties).

Press **apple pips** against your cheek, naming a possible partner with each one. The pip that sticks in place longest represents the one you will marry.

Put a **pip** by the fire. If it 'bounces and flies', bursting in the heat of the fire, your lover is faithful, but not so if the pip quietly burns away. However, if you live in Sussex the omens are quite the opposite – a popping pip foretells a break-up, whereas one which burns quietly means a steady courtship and a happy ending.

Put two **apple pips** (or two **ivy leaves** – a pointed one for a man and a rounded one for a woman) on top of a hot stove, naming one pip for yourself and one for your lover. If your pip moves towards the other, you are more fond of your lover than vice versa. If both the pips, or leaves, jump towards each other, you will marry each other, but if they jump apart you will quarrel and part. (The same omens can be drawn from two **acorns** dropped into a bowl of water.) Or put two **grains** on a shovel and place it on the fire. If both grains jump off together into the fire, they are 'bounding into matrimony' (which, some would say, is a pretty good representation of marriage!).

A group of unmarried people can tie **apples on strings** – one for each person – and twirl them around in front of the fire. If your apple is the first to fall off its string, you'll be the first in the group to wed, but if your apple is the last you are destined never to marry at all.

Hallowe'en also used to be known as **Nutcracker Night**. Take two **hazelnuts**, naming one for yourself and one for your lover, and put them side by side on the grate. If they fail to burn, or if they fly apart, your lover is unfaithful, but if they burn steadily together all is well. Or throw one nut into the fire and make a silent wish. The wish will come true if the nut catches fire.

If you find a 'lucky' **double-kernelled hazelnut**, you can make a wish while eating one kernel and throwing the other over your left shoulder, all in complete silence. Do not speak until someone asks you a question to which you can correctly answer yes. Alternatively, you can give an unsuspecting potential partner one kernel to eat while you eat the other. If you both remain silent until the nuts have been eaten, you will gain that person's friendship or love.

If a **live coal** falls out of the fire and lands near someone's feet, a wedding is presaged – either that of the person or of someone else in the house at the time. The **ashes** of a fire used to be scattered along a lane at Hallowe'en by a young man in the belief that the first girl to follow the trail would become his wife.

A sprig of **rosemary** placed under your pillow with a silver sixpence, if you can find such a coin, will bring you dreams of your future partner.

NATURE'S WAY

Going 'a-nutting' in Germany used to be a euphemism for love-making and groups of young people would go a-nutting on Holy Rood Day (14th September).

Ash trees were particularly honoured in mythology, often as the progenitors of mankind. For example, in Nordic mythology the first man was not Adam, but **Askr**, fashioned when the gods blew the breath of life into an ash. (The first woman was made from an alder tree.)

Ash leaves grow as several leaflets on a stem and it is rare – and very lucky – to find one with an equal number of leaflets on each side. A Northumberland girl would put such a lucky leaf in her left shoe in the belief that the first man she met after doing so would one day become her lover, however unlikely the prospect at the time they met. Similarly, a girl would tuck a **four-leaf clover** into her right shoe – the first man she met (or one with the same initial as his) was supposedly her future husband. A Yorkshire girl would tuck lucky ash leaves under her pillow to dream of her future husband that night, whilst to see a **clover leaf** in her dreams, four-leaved or not, foretold of a happy and prosperous marriage.

In Herefordshire, if a girl wanted to dream of her future husband, she would pick a sprig of **yew** from a churchyard which she had never visited before, and put it under her pillow; or gather nine **she-holly leaves** (variegated leaves with smooth edges) at midnight on a Friday, in silence, and tie them with nine knots in a triangular kerchief, maintaining complete silence until dawn.

In the West Country, **nine-banded ash faggots** (bundles of twigs bound with nine rods of ash or willow) were ceremonially burned like a Yule log on Christmas Eve. Unmarried girls living in the same household would name one of the bands for themselves, and the band which broke first on the fire prophesied who would be first to marry.

Willow played a role in divination too. In north-east England, a girl would take a willow branch in her left hand and run around the house three times trying to remain unseen. On her third circuit, the apparition of her future husband was supposed to be seen grasping the other end of the branch.

If she wasn't exhausted from all that running, a girl could cut a full-grown **bracken stem** near its base, at any time, and look at the characteristic markings revealed – they were the initials of the person she was said to be destined to marry.

Herbs have always been used in divination rituals and provided another way for a girl to see into the future.

Myrtle is traditionally associated with love, marriage and fertility – a sprig was placed in the girl's Prayer Book (in the section for the marriage service, where it says 'Wilt thou . . .') and the book put under her pillow for the night. If the myrtle had vanished by morning, her lover would marry her.

Sage is yet more powerful in foretelling the future. At midnight on Christmas Eve (or precisely at noon on St Mark's Eve, 24th April) pick a sage leaf each time the clock chimes, making sure none of them breaks. Your future marriage partner will then be seen behind you.

FLOWER POWER

Pick a **rosebud** on Midsummer Day (24th June), wrap it in white paper and store it secretly until Christmas Day. If it is still fresh and sweet, wear it to church that day – the man destined to marry you will come and take it away from you. If the rosebud has turned brown in the meantime – oh dear!

To dream of **red roses** foretells of luck in love (the rose is very much a love symbol).

Very early in the morning on May Day (1st May), Norfolk girls would gather bunches of **hawthorn blossom** for luck, bringing them home in absolute silence. If they spoke to anyone on the way home, they would not marry that year.

St John's Eve (23rd June) was another occasion for an early rise. Girls would be up before the dew had gone, gathering the yellow flowers of **St John's wort** (hypericum) to ensure that they married within the year.

St John's plant was **orpine**, also known as Live Long because it stays green for a long time after being cut, or as Midsummer Men because of its old use in love divinations. On Midsummer Eve a girl would fix a stem of orpine in clay on a shell, a slate, a piece of broken pottery or perhaps in a crack in the door and check it the following morning to see if it had inclined to the right, in which case her lover was faithful. (Woe betide him if it leaned to the left!) Alternatively, she would use two pieces, naming one for her lover and the other for herself, hoping she would find them leaning towards each other as a sign of good luck in their affair.

THE FOOD OF LOVE

Even the humble **onion** has a part to play in marriage divination. If you are spoilt for choice, scratch the name of each suitor on a different onion and put the bulbs in a warm place. The suitor named on the first onion to sprout is the one you should choose.

Peas are versatile fortune-tellers. If a girl found a pod containing nine perfect peas, she would leave it on the lintel of an outside door. The first man to cross that threshold was supposedly her future husband.

On the fifth Sunday in Lent, known locally as Carling Sunday, the traditional north England dish was carlings (grey peas) fried in butter. In Northumberland everyone helped themselves to a spoonful in turn until just a few peas remained in the dish, then these were removed, one by one, and whoever took the last pea would be the first to wed.

Then, of course, there are **cherry stones** (or prunes or whatever stoned fruit you have eaten) and the old rhymes 'This year, next year, some-time, never', for *when* you will marry, and 'Tinker, tailor, soldier, sailor, rich man, poor man, beggar man, thief' for the *type* of man you will marry.

SOWING THE SEEDS

Seeds and grains are often used in divination, and naturally have strong associations with human fer-tility and with riches to come, in marriage or otherwise. Some of these rituals were far from straightforward! For example, **fern seed** or bracken spores were said to make the gatherers invisible and give them control over all living things, including those they loved in vain.

However, the gathering of the seed was difficult and dangerous. It was said that the plant flowered only on Midsummer Eve and produced its seed instantly – it had to be collected that very night, strictly during the hour before midnight. The plant could not be touched with bare hands, so a forked hazel twig had to be used to bend it over and let the seeds fall into a white cloth, a pewter dish or an open Bible, with care being taken not to shake the plant (it had to yield its seed voluntarily).

ANIMAL MAGIC

In days of yore, would-be lovers put **wheat grains** in a circle, named each one for a different letter of the alphabet, and placed a **cockerel** in the middle. It was said to spell out the name of the potential partner by pecking one grain after another.

In Lincolnshire, the first **pancake** made on Shrove Tuesday was given to the barnyard cock – the number of hens that came to help him eat it represented the number of months before a daughter of the household would marry.

If you would rather eat the wretched bird, use the **wishbone**, or 'merrythought', to make your wish in the traditional way or, if you don't mind

Don't bring peacock feathers into the house if you have an unmarried daughter there - she will never marry.

making a fool of yourself, drill a small hole through the flat part that joins the two legs of the bone and then perch it on the bridge of your nose. Try to thread the hole like the eye of a needle. The number of unsuccessful attempts you make foretells the number of years before you will marry.

The **cuckoo** is also a useful divination bird for lovers. On hearing the first cuckoo in spring, an unmarried girl would turn round three times and then remove her left stocking (or the right one, if she was Irish). It was said that she would find a hair on the sole of her foot indicating the hair colour of her future mate. If she counted the number of notes when the first cuckoo called she could also tell how far off her marriage would be.

If a **ladybird** lands on your hand, very gently blow it away – it will fly off in the direction where your beloved lives. Watch out for **bees**, however – if they nest on the roof of a house, the unmarried daughter residing there will stay that way. But, if the household has a lucky black **cat**, there will be no lack of lovers for the lasses within.

FOOD FOR THOUGHT

From birds to eggs: take a newlaid **egg** at Hallowe'en, or some other significant eve, and prick its narrow end to let three drops of eggwhite fall into a basin of water. If you have the gift of imagination, you will be able to divine information from the shape it forms in the water, perhaps about your future partner or the number of children you will have.

The ritual of the **dumb cake** was rather more complicated. Having chosen an appropriate eve (Christmas Eve was the most popular), a girl would fast all day and observe silence until the ritual was completed. This entailed making a cake of flour, spring water, eggs and salt and pricking it with her initials, ensuring that an outside door or window remained open all the while. Having finished, she left the cake on the hearthstone, ready for her future husband's 'fetch' (double) to collect it on the stroke of midnight. Alternatively,

she would eat the cake and then, with clothes loosened, walk backwards upstairs to bed. It was said that the apparition of her future husband would chase her and grab at her clothes!

DESPERATE MEASURES

To reveal what the future held, a girl might have turned to *The Bible*. She put an iron door-key in the *Song of Solomon* or the *Book of Ruth*, with the ring of the key protruding, then bound the book tightly with her right garter. She then supported the book by putting the third finger of each hand under the key's ring and recited a special verse. If the book turned or fell to the ground during the recitation, she would marry; if it did not, she never would. If it turned to the right, her lover was faithful, but he was untrue if it turned to the left. To discover the initials of her future partner, she would recite the letters of the alphabet after the verse – the book would turn when she reached the initial of his Christian name.

If your future is not to be found in books, try the **stars**. Count exactly seven stars on seven successive nights. On the eighth day, the first person of the opposite sex who shakes your hand will marry you one day.

Or try catching the reflection of the new year's first **moon** in a bucket of water. Then look at the reflection through a new silk handkerchief or a piece of glass. You will see several moons, and the number you see represents the number of years until your wedding day. Or, on the night of a full moon, go and stand on a stone where you have never stood before, with your back to the moon, and look at its reflection in a handheld mirror – again you should see a number of smaller 'moons' in the glass, each representing a year before your wedding.

To be sure of marriage eventually, always remember to turn your **bed** from foot to head if you live in Oxfordshire, but never turn the mattress on a Friday if you live in Herefordshire because that will drive your sweetheart away.

Don't pick up a bent yellow **pin** in Sussex if you'd rather not be an old maid.

Wherever you are, if you have had to attend three **funerals** in a row, make sure that you attend a wedding ceremony before going to a fourth funeral, or you will never marry.

THE CHINESE WAY

Some people consult the stars to see if they and their prospective partners are compatible for marriage. The Chinese Zodiac is based on 12 **animal** signs – one for each of 12 consecutive years – and a person is influenced by the animal assigned to the birth-year, in contrast to the typical Western horoscope where the main influence is the *time* of year that you were born. In addition to the 12 animals, there are five **elements** (wood, fire, earth, metal and water) linked with the planets (Jupiter, Mars, Saturn, Venus and Mercury respectively). The combination of the animals and the elements thus gives a 60-year cycle in the Chinese lunar calendar in which each animal sign is combined with each element at some stage. The elements themselves are divided into two magnetic poles – the negative, **Yin**, and the positive, **Yang**.

The lunar year is divided into 12 months, each lasting 29.5 days (with a leap year every three years). Each day in the lunar calendar begins at 11pm and is divided into two-hour sections, each ruled by one of the animal signs. The sign which rules at the exact time of your birth has a strong influence on your personality.

To decide on compatibility with a partner you need to know the animal sign of the year of your birth, the lunar sign ruling at the hour of your birth, the moon sign that corresponds with your sun sign, the element of the year of your birth, and the fixed element of your animal sign. With the same information about your prospective partner, and no doubt a computer, you will be able to divine how well the relationship is likely to succeed! Oh, and you also need to know whether your element's pole is Yin or Yang, and that the animal years do not begin on 1st January but on different dates every year during January or February. There is a Chinese 10 000 Years (Perpetual) Lunar Calendar if you want to check see table below.

Very crudely, then, there are 144 possible marriage combinations based simply on the year of birth, and certainly not enough space here to tell you all about them, but the following are perhaps some of the best and worst partnerships, giving the husband's sign first:

Good:

Rat with Ox or Dragon
Ox with Rat, Snake or Rooster
Tiger with Horse, Dog or Boar
Rabbit with Rat, Dragon, Dog or Boar
Dragon with Rat, Monkey or Boar
Snake with Rat, Ox or Rooster
Horse with Tiger, Sheep or Dog
Sheep with Rabbit, Horse or Boar
Monkey with Rat, Dragon or Dog
Rooster with Ox, Dragon or Snake
Dog with Tiger, Rabbit or Horse
Boar with Tiger, Rabbit or Sheep

RAT	1900	1912	1924	1936	1948	1960	1972	1984
OX	1901	1913	1925	1937	1949	1961	1973	1985
TIGER	1902	1914	1926	1938	1950	1962	1974	1986
RABBIT	1903	1915	1927	1939	1951	1963	1975	1987
DRAGON	1904	1916	1928	1940	1952	1964	1976	1988
SNAKE	1905	1917	1929	1941	1953	1965	1977	1989
HORSE	1906	1918	1930	1942	1954	1966	1978	1990
SHEEP	1907	1919	1931	1943	1955	1967	1979	1991
MONKEY	1908	1920	1932	1944	1956	1968	1980	1992
ROOSTER	1909	1921	1933	1945	1957	1969	1981	1993
DOG	1910	1922	1934	1946	1958	1970	1982	1994
BOAR	1911	1923	1935	1947	1959	1971	1983	1995

Bad (or challenging!):

Rat with Horse, Sheep or Rooster
Ox with Tiger or Horse
Tiger with Rat, Ox, Rabbit, Snake, Monkey or
    Rooster!
Rabbit with Horse or Rooster
Dragon with Dog or Dragon

Snake with Tiger, Horse, Monkey or Boar
Horse with Ox or Rabbit
Sheep with Ox or Tiger
Monkey with Ox, Tiger or Rooster
Rooster with Rat, Rabbit or Horse
Dog with Dragon or Sheep
Boar with Snake

MAY DAY

Historically, May is the month dedicated to free and erotic lovemaking, dancing and general merriment in the open air, but it is a bad month for marriages in that it represents the antithesis of home life and conjugal bliss. The emphasis in May is on extramarital affairs and the first day of the month is by tradition the first day of summer – a day for lovers.

In the Ancient Roman Empire there was a great festival for **Cybele**, a Phrygian goddess of fertility and love – especially love *outside* marriage. The people honoured her on May Day, which also fell within the period of classical Roman festivals for **Flora**, goddess of flowers and fruit (28th April–3rd May). On May Day itself, Roman youths would honour Flora by heading for the fields for a day of dancing and singing in the fresh air, and probably much else besides. But during May the

The English May Day in medieval times was devoted to sport and games of all kinds. Archery became a particular favourite, and by the 16th century May Day had become known as Robin Hood's Day. Robin, as Lord of the May, soon 'adopted' the Queen of the May, Maid Marian, who was a character in the old May games and morris dances.

The real Robin Hood was Robert Fitzooth, born in about 1160 at Locksley, Nottinghamshire. He eventually died in 1247, when his cousin, the prioress of Kirklee nunnery in Yorkshire, allowed him to bleed to death during a blood-letting he had sought to relieve sickness. What an end for a romantic hero!

In China, spring is the time for love but not for marriage. In early spring the young Chinese, like young Europeans, would head for the woods to pick flowers and make love. Spring is the time for youth and betrothals, and as it turns to summer those who are still unattached are encouraged to commit themselves to marriage. In the Chinese spring, the girls play the leading role and find themselves attracted by the boys but, traditionally, autumn is the time for men to dominate, and is the time of home-making and maturity, a time when young men are attracted to the girls 'as though each of them in turn feeling his nature to be incomplete was suddenly seized with the irresistible desire to perfect it'. (Alwyn and Brinley Rees, *Celtic Heritage*)

Romans also held festivals for the goddess of chastity, Bona Dea, and that might be the *original* reason why May is considered an unlucky month for weddings.

In **England**, and throughout much of Europe, young girls rose at dawn to bathe naked in the early morning dew (dew is associated with virginity) as a beauty treatment in preparation for the lovers' day, or perhaps as a natural cold shower on the morning after the night before.

In the 16th century, May Eve was celebrated by large mixed groups which gathered in the woods for all-night open-air 'pastimes' and extramarital lovemaking. It was a time for frolicking under the shelter of birch trees, and wreaths of birch were exchanged as love tokens.

The morning of the first day of May was also the time when everybody went '**a-Maying**', gathering fresh flowers and branches from the hawthorn (or may blossom) as decorations, and choosing the prettiest girl in the village as **Queen of the May**. Bonfires were lit and maypoles were danced around – all part of ancient nature-worshipping ceremonies. How odd that, in some places, this great festival of nature, lovemaking and beauty has become a day for military parades and political rallies!

ST AGNES

Some marriage divination rites are carried out on **St Agnes' Eve** (20th January). Agnes, a Roman Christian, was martyred when she was only 12 or 13 years old, in about AD 304. She is the patron saint of young virgins – she rejected all her suitors, vowing that her body was consecrated to Christ. Most of the St Agnes' Eve divinations concern taking certain measures to ensure that you dream of your future marriage partner. As Keats divulged in his poem, 'The Eve of St Agnes', on St Agnes' Eve young virgins retired supperless after performing their rites, that they 'might have visions of delight, / And soft adorings from their loves receive / Upon the honey'd middle of the night'. Tennyson also wrote a poem with the same title.

ST VALENTINE'S DAY

All lovers know that **St Valentine's Day** is 14th February, a time for anonymous declarations of love. There are several saints called Valentine but none is really appropriate for a lovers' day – they were all firmly celibate! It is probably by chance that two of them (one a Roman priest and the other a bishop of Terni, both martyred towards the end of the 3rd century) have their feastday on 14th February. The romantic connection is with the Ancient Roman festival of the **Lupercalia** on 15th February, when girls and youths drew lots for each other. Lot-drawing was still a popular St Valentine's Day custom in England as late as 1700.

St Valentine's Day is closely associated with the mating season for birds, but a girl should be careful about which species of bird she first sees on the day – it represents the occupation or nature of her future husband:

ROBIN: sailor
BLACKBIRD: clergyman
GOLDFINCH: rich man
DOVE: good man
BLUE TIT: happy man
CROSSBILL: argumentative man
WOODPECKER: no man at all!

A Victorian valentine card – all lace and sentiment.

Girls, be careful about the first person you meet on the morning of St Valentine's Day – you will marry the first **bachelor** you see, so shut your eyes until you sense that Mr Right is around.

Today the fashion is to send **Valentine cards**, roses, chocolates and so on, and to publish messages in a newspaper – as corny or as sickly sentimental as desired – but this is always done anonymously, or at least under the guise of a pet nickname. The usually sober *Times* prints several pages of such messages on 14th February.

Cards, homemade and anonymously sent, first became popular in the late 18th century, and the Victorians developed a fine line in excessively sentimental and lace-trimmed affairs.

Long before cards, however, there were customs such as carrying a flaming **brandon** or Cupid's torch for your loved one (hence the phrase 'carrying a torch' for someone). Then came the general custom of giving (or soliciting!) Valentine **presents**. Devonian girls would approach the young men of their choice and recite a little rhyme

which requested them to buy each a pair of **gloves** as an Easter present. If the girl wore the gloves to church on Easter Sunday, it boded well for the courtship. (Another glove tradition – if a woman finds a man asleep in his chair, she can claim a pair of gloves as forfeit if she wakes him with a kiss.)

While today hopeful lovers might be disappointed at a lack of Valentine cards (reassuring themselves that their love is strong enough not to need such fripperies, perhaps), not so long ago a girl who had not been kissed on St Valentine's Day, or even visited by a young man, would suffer the further humiliation of being treated like a jilted woman and was traditionally rubbed down with **pea-straw** (the dead part of the plant) by the local lads.

LOVE AMONG THE GODS

Most true love stories are variations on mythological themes. The gods and goddesses of the ancients seemed to spend a great deal of their time dallying with lovers, often mortal rather than immortal, and usually with disastrous consequences for the mortals. Goddesses in particular often seemed to be spiteful, frequently seeking revenge if a mortal woman was more beautiful than they or attracted the love of the god or mortal man with whom the goddess was in love.

Venus was the Roman goddess of love and beauty (her Greek equivalent was **Aphrodite**). She was the daughter of Jupiter and Dione and was married to the lame iron-forger, Vulcan, but she had many, many lovers and wore a special love-girdle (*Cestus*), which had the magical power to incite passionate love and fell off when she 'wantoned with Mars'. Irresistible women were said to be wearing Venus's girdle. Her flowers were **myrtle** and **rose**, her favourite birds the **swan** and the **dove**.

The Venusberg, or Horselberg, is the mountain of love and delight between Eisenach and Gotha in Germany. According to German legend, Venus used to hold court in its caverns but rarely allowed human visitors. The symbolism is obvious.

Venus gave her name to the second planet from the sun which, in **astrology**, 'signifiethe white men or browne . . . joyfull, laughter, liberal, pleasers, dauncers, entertayners of women, players, perfumers, musitions, messengers of love', which sums up what the goddess represents. The astronomical symbol of the planet Venus is a mirror.

Rather surprisingly in view of her passion for love affairs with gods and mortals, Venus was worshipped as a symbol of **marriage** and motherhood. **Caesar** erected a temple to her as *Venus Genetrix* ('she who has borne') in the Forum, in Rome, and similar statues show her lifting her clothes and holding an apple as an emblem of fecundity. She was also known as *Venus Verticordia*, the name meaning 'turner of hearts', when she was invoked to turn the hearts of women to virtue and chastity. Above all, she is represented in art as an exceedingly beautiful woman.

Cupid was Venus's son by the god **Mercury**. He was the god of love (called **Eros** in Greek) and he induced love by shooting arrows at his victims – gold ones to inspire virtuous love and lead ones for sensual love. Cupid is usually represented as a fat little boy with wings who is Venus's constant companion, always doing her bidding, but one of the most beautiful love stories in mythology concerns the adult Cupid . . .

Psyche (whose name means 'soul' in Greek, and also implies the freedom of a butterfly) was so beautiful that Venus became jealous and instructed Cupid to fill the innocent girl with desire for a 'low, mean, unworthy being'. Cupid began to carry out his task but fell in love with her himself (he pricked himself with his own arrow by mistake). Psyche remained beautiful but found that her beauty did not inspire love in men and she

Cybele was a Phrygian goddess of love in Roman Europe and was the patroness of love *outside* marriage – hence her association with May, the first month of summer and the month of free and extramarital love.

seemed destined to become a lonely old maid. However, a fortune-teller informed her parents of Venus's anger and said that the girl was destined to be the bride of no mortal lover – that her future husband was a monster living at the top of a mountain. Psyche faced her fate boldly and went to the mountain where she was welcomed into a delightful palace and her every need was attended to by invisible servants. Her husband, too, remained unseen and came to her only under the cover of darkness, but he was so loving and gentle that she soon returned his passion.

However, he would never let her see him. 'Why should you wish to behold me?' he asked. 'Have you any doubt of my love? Have you any wish ungratified? If you saw me, perhaps you would fear me, perhaps adore me, but all I ask of you is to love me. I would rather you would love me as an equal than adore me as a god.'

The story is a long one but, to cut it short, Psyche's sisters persuaded her to take a lamplight look at the monster. To her surprise, he was the most beautiful man she had ever seen, but he woke as she looked, and vanished. He was, of course, Cupid. She tried to follow him but stumbled and, pitying her, he paused to admonish her gently for failing to trust him and said that her punishment would be that he would leave her forever, because 'love cannot dwell with suspicion'.

Psyche wandered far and wide in search of him, while Venus, still spiteful, set her endless impossible tasks. Nevertheless, Cupid watched over her, unknown to either, and sent unlikely helpers when she needed them. The tasks became increasingly dangerous but she persisted, until Cupid, having already secretly rescued her from danger, could no longer bear their separation and persuaded the gods (including Venus) to let him be joined with Psyche in perpetuity as an immortal.

The Greek equivalent of Venus is **Aphrodite** (the name means 'born of the sea-foam'), who was the goddess of flowering nature as well as love, though she was married to the war god **Ares**. Her particular paramour was the beautiful young **Adonis**, who was eventually killed by a wild boar, but Aphrodite turned his spilt blood into the flowers of the **anemone**. At the shrine of Aphrodite, women worshippers willingly gave themselves to strangers . . .

L'Amour et Psyché *by Delaistre. Psyché uses a lamp to steal a look at her shy new husband while he sleeps.*

A sarcophagus relief of a classical marriage ceremony. The couple are attended by the luck-bringing deities of Valour, Success, and Good Fortune.

Juno, wife and sister of Jupiter and the queen of heaven in Roman mythology (her Greek equivalent was Hera), was the special protectress of women and of marriage but she was also a war goddess! She was the woman's equivalent of a man's 'genius', which was a guardian spirit that for his whole lifetime governed his fortunes and his character, and essentially wanted him to enjoy life's pleasures.

Freyja (also known as Frigg) was the Scandinavian goddess of sexual love, fertility, marriage and, incongruously, the dead. She was the wife of Odin and the highest ranking of the goddesses. She loved music, flowers, the spring and love-songs, and her chariot was drawn by cats. Norsemen regarded Friday as the luckiest day of the week, perfect for weddings, because it was named after her.

Pyramus and **Thisbe**, much mocked in Shake-speare's *A Midsummer Night's Dream*, were the lovers in a Babylonian tragedy. Their parents lived next door to each other in semi-detached houses and it was a typical case of a girl falling in love with the boy next door. The parents forbade the romance but the couple discovered a hole in the party wall for passing secret messages. The tragic ending, full of misunderstandings, smacks of *Romeo and Juliet*.

Ancient Greek lovers, **Hero** and **Leander** were separated not by a wall but by a mile of water with strong currents – they lived on opposite sides of the Hellespont, one in Asia and one in Europe. Every night Hero swam across to meet his lover until he was drowned one night in a storm. Lord

Pachamama is the earth mother goddess in Bolivia. The sowing of seed in her belly is a ritual act performed by the men and women of the farming communities. Survival and human fertility are seen as inextricably bound up with nature, and the Aymara Indians say that everything in this world comes in pairs, so that men and women have complementary roles in the countryside. By uniting as a couple (legally or not), the man and woman become recognised as adults and as a single cultural and social unit combining their contrasting natures. Man is fire, heat, lightning and power; woman is dark, negative, hidden, archaic and wild.

Bolivian courtship rituals have many links with this bond with the earth. 'Romantic' overtures include throwing pebbles at each other over a wall, flashing sunlight in the beloved's face with a mirror from a distance, snatching and hiding his or her hat or tugging a woman's shawl roughly in passing. Direct contact between adolescents is taboo, hence the use of pebbles to contact the beloved's body indirectly and the grabbing of outer clothing in the hope that the loved one will visit your home to retrieve the hat or shawl. This tantalising courtship game can go on for weeks, often reaching its climax at a fiesta where alcohol flows freely, and a girl might be 'captured' by her suitor and taken to his home for the night. The very next morning her parents will begin negotiations with his parents to 'regularise' the relationship.

Byron, the 19th-century poet, tried the same swim to prove that it was possible – it was, but it was a tremendous test of skill and strength. Oh, the power of love!

In India, the **Divine Woman** was the idealisation of adulterous love. During the 7th and 8th centuries, in the Courts of Love in Bengal, the adherents of conjugal love always lost their cases to those who upheld adultery. It was said that a woman was never without a husband – until she was four years old she was the wife of the moon spirit, Candra, then successively the air spirit, Gandharva (her supernatural suitor for life, half man and half bird, whose presence was thought essential to conception) and the fire spirit, Agni, then finally her human husband.

There is an Indian legend about a king called **Pururavas,** who was married to **Urvashi** on condition that he embraced her three times every day but never against her will, and that she should never have to see him naked. Her Gandharva wanted her back after a while and tricked the couple by stealing her pet lambs so that Pururavas leaped out of bed to chase them and his wife, caught by surprise, saw him naked and promptly vanished. (There is a 'happily ever after' ending to this very long story.)

King Arthur's marriage to Guinever was carefully arranged by the magician, Merlin, but his party went to her father incognito and they found themselves having to help him win a battle against an Irish king. Covered in glory after the fight, they eventually revealed themselves. Guinever, however, had already fallen in love with the unknown hero and they had a splendid seven-day wedding festival, interrupted by the enemy's reappearance so that the battle recommenced. Guinever should have realised what sort of a man she was marrying and it is little wonder that she later sought solace in the arms of the good knight, Launcelot, who first saw her when he was 18 and immediately became devoted, remaining so for the rest of his life – he died of grief six weeks after her death.

King Arthur's gallant nephew, Sir Gawain, once rescued his uncle by marrying an exceptionally hideous hag – his noble gesture actually turned her back into the lovely woman she really was. Think of the princess who kissed the frog . . .

VIRGINITY

In many cultures, especially those in India, a virgin bride is desirable, often essential, and can attract a higher brideprice, but in others quite the opposite is true. In fact, a woman's ability to bear children is so crucial that the most favoured brides are already pregnant, or have proved their fertility by having borne at least one child before marriage, by someone other than their husband if necessary.

Within the cultures that prize it, there are many symbols connected with virginity. **Dew** symbolises the precious and ephemeral while white flowers, such as **orange blossom**, symbolise innocence. A man who treads on **white lilies** is thought to defile the purity of his women.

The **unicorn** is a fabled beast – a white horse with the legs of a deer, the tail of a lion and a single long spiralling horn growing from its forehead. It is

In the 18th century, a man living in Portland, Dorset, would separate from his girlfriend if she was not pregnant after what he considered to be a reasonable term of courtship.

said to be so vicious that only a virgin can catch it. Having been caught, it will lie down at her feet – the symbolism speaks for itself.

A girl or woman of untainted reputation who died a virgin used to be honoured with a special **maiden's garland** of white linen sprinkled with white and coloured rosettes and streamers, with a symbolic white glove hanging at the centre. At her funeral, the garland was carried by young people

Rinoceron ū virgini se inclinare valet. Cur · verbum patris celica virgo nō generaret · Ysi· simul et ·Alanus·:–

Unicorn and Virgin – the mythical and vicious unicorn could only be tamed by a virgin.

In Northumberland, sole ownership of hive bees was considered unlucky. It was thought that a co-ownership, ideally between a man from one household and a woman from another, was far luckier.

dressed in white in procession ahead of her coffin. Afterwards, the garland was hung in the church over her usual seat in the chancel for a certain period, in case anyone wanted to challenge her right to be so honoured. Later, it was suspended permanently in another part of the church and the pieces which gradually fell off were properly buried in the churchyard. It was very unlucky to remove the garland or throw it away in the meantime.

Traditionally, **bees** are said to abhor unchastity and have the ability to detect it in a person. Even when no one in the family is aware of the transgression the bees will attack the guilty! One sign of virginity, therefore, was that a girl could walk

In 1990 an Asian bride, Zahida Seemi, now 30 years old, was awarded damages for slander to the tune of £20 000 against her husband, who had suggested that she was not a virgin when they had married in 1981. On their wedding night he told her that she had been associating with other men but that he would consider keeping her if her parents produced 100 000 rupees (about £3500). They had married in England (the bridegroom was living in Chigwell, Essex, at the time) and then returned to Pakistan, where it seems that his family spread the rumours about her being 'a woman, not a girl'. Consequently, her husband refused to consummate the marriage. They divorced soon afterwards, but in 1985 doctors were able to prove that she was indeed still a virgin. She won back her good reputation through the High Court in England under the Slander of Women Act, 1891.

through a swarm without being stung.

In the days when child marriages were commonplace among **Hindus**, the question of bridal virginity never arose – the couple were married before puberty. However, virginity is still highly prized in the Asian community in Britain today and Muslims, in particular, consider premarital sex a great sin.

If a **Wolof** tribeswoman in West Africa is declared a virgin on her wedding night, it is an excuse for additional feasting among the working groups of which the couple are members. During the festivities an elderly woman from the husband's compound checks nightly to see if the couple have had intercourse. If there is evidence of the bride's virginity, the bride can demand whatever she wishes as her reward for virtue. If the husband does not consummate the union until after the wedding festivities, the bride's kinsfolk can demand from him a goat, money for a second goat, 12 handfuls of grain and two bottles of palm oil so that they can prepare for yet another feast. Any excuse for a party!

The old **feudal system** in Europe allowed a lord to claim the maidenhead of the virgins on his estate and girls were considered honoured rather than disgraced by such attentions.

CHASTITY AND CELIBACY

Chastity is defined as sexual purity or virtue – the word comes from the Latin word for pure (*castus*).

Chastity is a necessary qualification for sainthood. **St Wilgefortis** was a Portuguese princess who was determined to remain a virgin, so she deliberately repelled her many suitors by praying for a beard. When she grew one, her furious father, or perhaps her disgusted suitor, the King of Sicily, had her crucified.

Vows of chastity prevented 11th-century monks from marrying, but in many places parish priests were not specifically banned from marriage. Bishops were allowed to marry once only as this was in accordance with *The Bible*. In 1 Timothy 3 v 2, St Paul is recorded as saying 'Now the overseer must be above reproach, the husband of but one wife.'

Celibacy is the unmarried state usually under a vow. The word comes from the Latin *caelebs*, meaning single.

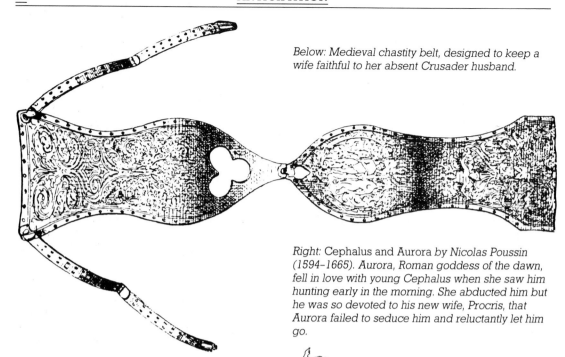

Below: Medieval chastity belt, designed to keep a wife faithful to her absent Crusader husband.

Right: Cephalus and Aurora by Nicolas Poussin (1594-1665). Aurora, Roman goddess of the dawn, fell in love with young Cephalus when she saw him hunting early in the morning. She abducted him but he was so devoted to his new wife, Procris, that Aurora failed to seduce him and reluctantly let him go.

The **Agapetae** of 3rd-century Greece were ascetic women who took a vow of virginity and then contracted a 'spiritual marriage' with monks. The movement became widespread and, inevitably in due course, scandalous because the women 'attended to the monks' needs'. It was condemned during the 4th century, but it was not totally suppressed until the Lateral Council of 1139.

In the **Baha'i** faith (which is now widespread, having broken away from Islam in the 19th century) monastic celibacy is forbidden, but chastity is essential and sex is permissible only within marriage.

The monks of **Iona**, whose monastery on the island was founded in AD 563 by Columba of Ireland, did not take monastic vows of celibacy and were allowed to marry. However, the wives did not live in the monastery but in an adjacent place, or on the nearby 'Island of Women' (*Eilen nam ban*) where their monastic husbands could live with them except when their duties required them to attend the sanctuary or school. Even today, in several cultures worldwide, the **longhouse** system is preferred. The men live in one building and the women in another, husbands and wives meeting only when it suits them to do so.

The last Pope to be married was Adrian II (867-72), but Pope Alexander VI fathered at least four children before he was elected Pope in 1492.

Pygmalion, in the original Greek myth, was King of Cyprus and was also a good sculptor. He thought that women caused far too much trouble in a man's life and he resolved to remain celibate and never marry. Instead he carved himself a beautiful ivory statue of a perfect woman and promptly fell in love with it. **Aphrodite**, the Greek goddess of love, kindly brought the statue to life so that he could marry her after all.

VIRGIN ON THE RIDICULOUS

In the Fens, single girls who had 'fallen' tried eating **parsley** three times a day for three weeks to remedy the situation. Men, however, had a different use for the plant. They ate parsley seeds before a drinking bout because it was said that the seed would help 'men that have weak brains' to hold their drink better.

The earliest meaning of a **grass widow** was an unmarried mother, no doubt in reference to the

grass stains on her clothes from making love in the fields. The term also referred to a discarded mistress.

In Wales, the sound of **owls** hooting continually is said to mean that a girl in the village is about to lose her virginity.

In parts of West Africa, a woman in an informal (ie unmarried) union continues to live in her mother's house, with her children. Her lover is expected to provide support but she has no recourse against him if he fails to do so.

In Sir Thomas More's *Utopia* (1518), a man or woman who was not a virgin at their own wedding was severely punished – and so was the householder in whose home the untoward conduct had occurred, as he was deemed to be guilty of carelessness.

SIMPLY CHARMING

Whenever personal charms have failed to captivate the beloved, love potions, spells and charms have been used. Beware! The trouble with wishes is that you must specify what you want . . . The Greek goddess of the dawn, **Aurora**, took a fancy to a mortal called **Tithonus** (son of the King of Troy). She persuaded Jupiter to grant the man immortality and whisk him heavenwards as her eternal lover, but she forgot to ask for the gift of eternal youth as well and when he grew old and feeble Aurora shut him away and eventually turned him into a grasshopper!

The **Fanti** tribe of Ghana use a *kwanga* charm to attract the opposite sex. It is a mixture which is applied to the hair after it has been concocted by a priest using secret magical ingredients. A European hairdressing pomade is now added to make the kwanga easier to apply – it also gives it an enticing perfume.

Mistletoe has always been considered a magical plant, flourishing without being in contact with the earth. It has different connotations in different cultures, including peace, welcome, protection (from thunderstorms and witches) and general healing. It is also regarded as a lucky charm, a pagan symbol, a sacred druidic plant, a fertility charm for cows and, uniquely among the English, an excuse for kissing. If a girl stands under the Christmas mistletoe bough she cannot refuse a kiss!

There are many ways of summoning an unwilling or wayward lover but they are not for the faint-hearted . . .

With a suitable chant, throw a dozen new **pins** into a fire at midnight, or push two pins into a

Parents of young girls used to ban honeysuckle or lime blossom from the house in case the heavy scent induced erotic dreams.

A man should prick the pits all over the skin of an orange and put it in his armpit overnight. The next day, he should give the orange to a girl he desires, without telling her where it has been or why he's offering it. If she eats the fruit, she will return his love.

lighted candle or a dead pigeon's heart. Perhaps you would prefer to hide a turtle dove's dried **tongue** under your loved one's pillow, or stick a knife into a **bone** from a roasted shoulder of lamb on three successive nights. You could gather three **roses** (symbols of love) on Midsummer Eve and, in the early hours of Midsummer Day, bury one of them under a yew and one in a fresh grave, keeping the third under your pillow for three nights before burning it. You will haunt your lover's dreams and he will be restless until he returns to you.

Are you doubtful of your lover's fidelity? Secretly dig up some earth from your beloved's footprint, put it in a flowerpot and sow some **marigold** seeds in it. He will stray no more. To retain love, give your lover a flowering sprig of **myrtle** or a drink of myrtle tea. Nicholas Culpepper, the 17th-century physican and herbalist, suggested that a man and wife should eat **periwinkle** (vinca) leaves together as it would 'cause love between them'.

'IN THE MOOD' FOOD

The flowering herb **valerian** is both a charm and an ingredient of many love potions, though it stinks like a tomcat (cats love it and so, oddly, do rats). In medieval times people liked the smell and often used it as a perfume, and in Wales they say that a girl who wears a sprig of valerian will never lack suitors.

Lettuce arouses love if you eat enough of it, but because of its sedative qualities, too much makes you sleepy – which might be just what your seducer intends! By contrast, the suggestively shaped roots of **bryony** make an excellent aphrodisiac but too much is over-exciting – and purgative. In the past, **cyclamen**, another purgative, was made into little aphrodisiac cakes.

Woe betide anyone who dug up the root of the **mandrake** – its screech was said to bring madness or even death to those who heard it. If they lived to tell the tale, this magical and suggestive root was

thought to compel love, prevent sterility and banish barrenness. **Ginseng** is another suggestive and supposedly love-enhancing root, likewise the 'dogstone' **orchis**.

The reputation of the **tomato** as an aphrodisiac was once so widespread that the Puritans labelled it as poisonous. It became known as the 'love apple' because the English thought that the French called it a *pomme d'amour* (apple of love). In fact it was *pomme du Moor* – it had come to France from South America via North Africa.

Fruit of most kinds can be sensual to eat and thus perhaps put people in the right frame of mind for making love, but even greater claims are made for some fruits, especially **fresh figs** and **pomegranates** (both full of seeds, which are equated with fertility) and, believe it or not, **prunes**.

Truffles apparently produce androstenol, which is a sexually stimulating scent – well, it interests sows.

Oysters have always been a favourite food for lovers because they contain dopamine, which is supposed to stimulate desire. Mind you, the chemical is also found in **broad beans** – not quite the same, is it?

Powdered **pearls** or **coral** were favoured by Cleopatra as aphrodisiacs, especially when crushed in wine.

A nutritionist in Brazil recently suggested that people should eat dead rats to stimulate the libido in cases of sexual dysfunction. Equally mouthwatering is the recommended dish of black ants marinaded in oil or honey.

Here are some more foods for lovers, claimed by some to be effective but with no guarantees:

Termites	Rattlesnake	Ginger
Fried cuttlefish	Celery	Saffron
Duck's beak	Young parsnips	Coriander
Leopard's heart	Spinach	Mint
Snails	Carrots	Basil
Alligator	Onions	Rosemary
Frog's legs	Garlic	Thyme
Bear's paws	Mangoes	Parsley
Curried fruitbat	Limes	Macaroni
Pig's trotters	Tangerines	Goat's milk
Dried beef	Apricots	Ass's milk
Blood puddings	Bananas	Rice in sheep's
Raw steak	Cinnamon	milk

A recipe for **bridescake**, published at the turn of the century:

1 lb of love	1 oz pounded wit
½lb butter of youth	1 oz dry humour
½lb good looks	2 tbsp sweet argument
1 lb sweet temper	1 pt rippling laughter
½lb blunder of faults	1½ wineglasses of
1 lb self-forgetfulness	common sense

Mix the love, looks and sweet temper into a well-furnished house; beat the butter to a cream; mix these ingredients well together with the blunder of faults and self-forgetfulness. Stir the pounded wit and dry humour with the sweet argument, then add to the above. Gently pour in the rippling laughter and common sense, and mix thoroughly. Bake well forever.

LOVE LOST

Sadly, not all love is built to last – things have a nasty habit of turning sour. Take heart, though, all you need is a little broken **crabshell**. Mixed into your ex-lover's food it should ensure that he pines for you throughout his new marriage (if he doesn't choke first, that is!). Or you might gain more satisfaction by plucking some **rue** from a churchyard and throwing it at the bounder as he emerges from the church with his new bride.

Jilted lovers used to wear **willow** garlands as symbols of grief, and some unkind people would send such a garland to a jilted person when the former lover found someone new. Even more spitefully, others would send a peeled **hazel twig** (the 'white stick') and a piece of **ginger**, with a mocking verse attached.

On May Day in some parts of Wales, a girl who had jilted her lover might find a mocking **straw effigy** or even a **horse's skull** tied to her door rather than a ribbon-tied bunch of flowers. A prude suffered similar insults – she, like the jilter, was labelled 'unloving', and that is a crime in the month of May!

In some cultures, the belief in the power of love charms is so strong that an errant husband is automatically forgiven. After all, the poor man has been bewitched and can't help himself. Some wives certainly *do* understand their husbands!

THE LANGUAGE OF FLOWERS

Worldwide, flowers are symbols of love and fertility, and in the language of love every flower has its own significance. This was especially true in Victorian times, when symbolism was preferable to bold declaration. Here is an American 'Floral Vocabulary' published in 1845 – in a farming magazine!

ACACIA (Yellow): Concealed love
ACACIA (Rose): Elegance
ACALEA: Temperance
ACANTHUS: The Arts
ACONITE-LEAVED CROWFOOT: Lustre
AGNUS CASTUS: Coldness without love
AGRIMONY: Thankfulness
ALMOND BLOSSOM: Hope
ALOE: Bitterness
ALTHEA FURTEX: Consumed by love
ALYSSUM: Worth beyond beauty
AMARANTH: Immortality
AMARYLLIS: Beautiful but timid
AMBROSIA: Returned affection
ANEMONE: Frailty
ANGELICA: Inspiration
APOCYNUM: Falsehood
APPLE BLOSSOM: Good and great
ARUM: Ferocity and deceit
ASH: Grandeur
ASPEN TREE: Sensibility
ASPHODEL: My regrets follow you
ASTER: Beauty in retirement
AURICULA (Scarlet): Pride
BACHELOR'S BUTTON: Hope in misery
BALM: Social intercourse
BALSAM: Impatience
BARBERRY: Sourness
BASIL: Hatred
BAY LEAF: I change but in dying
BAY WREATH: Reward of merit
BEECH: Prosperity
BETONY: Surprise
BINDWEED: Humility
BIRCH: Gracefulness
BLACK POPLAR: Courage
BLACKTHORN: Difficulty
BLUEBELL: Constancy

BORAGE: Bluntness
BOX: Stoicism
BROOM: Neatness
BUCKBEAN: Calm repose
BURDOCK: Importunity
BUTTERCUP: Ingratitude
CALLA: Feminine modesty
CALYCANTHUS: Benevolence
CANDYTUFT: Indifference
CANTERBURY BELL: Gratitude
CARDINAL FLOWER: Distinction
CARNATION: Disdain
CATCH-FLY: Artifice
CEDAR TREE: Strength
CHAMOMILE: Energy
CHERRY BLOSSOM: Spiritual beauty
CHESTNUT: Render me justice
CHINA ASTER: Variety
CHINA PINK: Aversion
CHRYSANTHEMUM: Cheerfulness
CLEMATIS: Mental beauty
COLTSFOOT: Maternal care
COLUMBINE: Half folly
COREOPSIS: Ever cheerful
CORIANDER: Concealed worth
COWSLIP: Native grace
CROCUS: Youthful gladness
CROWN IMPERIAL: Majesty
CYPRESS: Mourning
DAFFODIL: Delusive hope
DAHLIA: Dignity and elegance
DAISY: Innocence
DANDELION: Oracle
DEWPLANT: Serenade
DOGWOOD: Durability
DRAGON PLANT: Snare
EGLANTINE: Poetry
ELDER: Compassion
ELM: Dignity
ENCHANTER'S NIGHTSHADE: Fascination
EVERGREEN: Poverty
EVERLASTING: Unceasing remembrance
FENNEL: Strength

FERN: Sincerity
FIR: Time
FLAX: Acknowledged kindness
FLOWERING REED: Confidence in heaven
FLOWER-OF-AN-HOUR: Delicate beauty
FORGET-ME-NOT: True love
FOXGLOVE: I am ambitious for your sake
FUCHSIA: Confiding love
GERANIUMS:
  (Ivy-leaved): Bridal favour
  (Lemon): A tranquil mind
  (Nutmeg): I shall meet you
  (Oak): True friendship
  (Rose): Preference
  (Scarlet): Consolation
  (Silver): Recall
GILLYFLOWER: Lasting beauty
GLORY FLOWER: Glorious beauty
GOLDENROD: Encouragement
GRAPE (Wild): Charity
GRASS: Utility
HAREBELL: Grief
HAWTHORN: Hope
HAZEL: Reconciliation
HEARTSEASE PANSY: Think of me
HEATH: Solitude
HELIOTROPE: Devotion
HELLEBORE: Calumny
HOLLYHOCK: Fruitfulness
HOPS: Injustice
HORNBEAM: Ornament
HORSE CHESTNUT: Luxuriancy
HOUSELEEK: Vivacity
HOUSTONIA: Content
HYACINTH: Game, play
HYDRANGEA: Heartlessness
ICELANDIC MOSS: Health
ICEPLANT: Your looks freeze me
IRIS: A message for you
IVY: Friendship
JASMINE (White): Amiability

JASMINE (Yellow): Elegant gracefulness
JONQUIL: Desire
JUDAS TREE: Unbelief
JUNIPER: Protection
KENNEDIA: Mental excellence
KINGCUP: I wish I was rich
LABURNUM: Pensive beauty
LADY'S SLIPPER: Capricious beauty
LARCH: Boldness
LARKSPUR: Fickleness
LAUREL: Glory
LAURUSTINUS: I die neglected
LAVENDER: Acknowledgement
LEMON BLOOM: Discretion
LETTUCE: Cold-hearted
LILAC: First emotions of love
LILY (White): Purity, modesty
LILY-OF-THE-VALLEY: Return of happiness
LINDEN TREE: Matrimony
LOBELIA: Malevolence
LOCUST-TREE: Affection beyond the grave
LONDON PRIDE: Frivolity
LOTUS: Estranged love
LOVE-IN-A-MIST: Perplexity
LOVE-IN-A-PUZZLE: Embarrassment
LOVE-LIES-BLEEDING: Hopeless, not heartless
LUCERN: Life
LUPIN: Sorrow, dejection
MADWORT (Rock): Tranquillity
MAGNOLIA: Love of nature
MAIZE: Plenty
MALLOW: Sweet disposition
MANDRAKE: Rarity
MAPLE: Reserve
MARIGOLD: Inquietude
MARVEL OF PERU: Timidity
MEADOW SAFFRON: My best days are past
MEADOWSWEET: Uselessness
MERCURY: Goodness
MEZEREON: Desire to please
MIGNONETTE: Excellence and loveliness
MIMOSA: Sensitiveness
MINT: Virtue
MISTLETOE: I surmount all obstacles
MOONWORT: Forgetfulness
MOSS (tuft of): Maternal love
MOTHERWORT: Secret love

MOUSE-EAR: Forget me not
MULBERRY TREE: Wisdom
MUSHROOM: Suspicion
MYRTLE: Love in absence
NARCISSUS: Egotism
NASTURTIUM: Patriotism
NETTLE: Slander
NIGHTBLOOMING CEREUS: Transient beauty
NIGHTSHADE: Dark thoughts
NOSEGAY: Gallantry
OAK: Hospitality
OATS: Music
OLEANDER: Beware
OLIVE BRANCH: Peace
ORANGE TREE: Generosity
ORCHIS: A belle
OSIER: Frankness
OX-EYE DAISY: Obstacle
PALM: Victory
PARSLEY: Entertainment
PASSIONFLOWER: Religious superstition
PEA (Everlasting): Wilt thou go with me?
PEA (Sweet): Departure
PEACH BLOSSOM: I am your captive
PENNYROYAL: Flee away
PEONY: Ostentation
PERIWINKLE: Sweet remembrances
PERUVIAN HELIOTROPE: Infatuation
PETUNIA: Thou art less proud than they deem thee
PHLOX: We are united
PIMPERNEL: Assignation
PINE: Pity
PINEAPPLE: You are perfect
PINK: Purity of affection
PLANE TREE: Genius
PLUM TREE: Keep your promises
POLYANTHUS: Confidence
POMEGRANATE: Foolishness
POPPY: Consolation of sleep
PRICKLY PEAR: Satire
PRIMROSE: Early youth
PRIMROSE (Evening): I am more constant than thou
PRIVET: Prohibition
PYRUS JAPONICA: Fairies' fire
QUAMOCLET: Busybody
QUEEN'S ROCKET: Queen of coquettes

RAGGED ROBIN: Dandy
ROSEBUD: A young girl
ROSEMARY: Remembrance
ROSES:
  (Austrian): Very lovely
  (Bridal): Simplicity and beauty
  (Burgundy): Simplicity and beauty
  (Damask): Bashful love
  (Monthly): Beauty ever new
  (Moss): Pleasure without alloy
  (Multiflora): Grace
  (Musk): Capricious beauty
  (White): Silent sadness
  (Yellow): Infidelity
RUE: Purification
RUSH: Docility
SAFFRON: Excess is dangerous
SAGE: Domestic virtues
SCABIOUS: Unfortunate attachment
SCARLET IPOMOEA: Attachment
SENSITIVE PLANT: Sensitiveness
SERPENTINE CACTUS: Horror
SNAPDRAGON: Presumption
SNOWBALL: Thoughts of heaven
SOUTHERNWOOD: Jesting
SPIDERWORT: Transient happiness
ST JOHN'S WORT: Animosity
STAR OF BETHLEHEM: The light of our path
STRAWBERRY: Perfect excellence
STRIPED PINK: Refusal
SUMACH: Splendour
SUNFLOWER: False riches
SWEETBRIER: Poetry
SWEET FLAG: Fitness
SWEET SULTAN: Felicity
SWEET-SCENTED TUSSILAGE: Justice shall be done you
SWEET WILLIAM: A smile
SYRINGA: Memory
TAMARISK: Crime
TANSY: Resistance
TEASEL: Misanthropy
THISTLE: I will never forget thee
THORNAPPLE: Deceitful charms
THYME: Activity
TREMELLA: Resistance
TRUMPET-FLOWER:

Separation	**(White):** Candour	**WHEAT:** Riches
TULIP: Declaration of love	**(Blue):** Modesty	**WINTERCHERRY:** Deception
VALERIAN: Accommodating	**(Yellow):** Rural happiness	**WITCH HAZEL:** A spell
disposition	**VIRGIN'S BOWER:** Filial love	**WOOD SORREL:** Joy
VENUS'S FLY-TRAP: Deceit	**WAKE-ROBIN:** Ardour	**WOODBINE:** Fraternal joy
VENUS'S LOOKING-GLASS:	**WALLFLOWER:** Fidelity in	**WORMWOOD:** Absence
Flattery	misfortune	**YARROW:** Thou alone canst cure
VERBENA: Sensibility	**WATERLILY:** Purity of heart	**YEW:** Sorrow
VINE: Intoxication	**WAXPLANT:** Susceptibility	**ZINNIA:** Absence
VIOLETS:	**WEEPING WILLOW:** Forsaken	

Traditionally, brides like to include symbolic flowers in their wedding bouquets. **Rosemary** represents fidelity. In the 17th century, brides wove rosemary flowers and leaves into their wedding wreaths, bridesmaids and groomsmen carried gilded branches of the plant, and it was dipped into the couple's wine before they drank to ensure happiness and the endurance of love.

Myrtle is the flower of Venus, the Roman goddess of love. It represents love and marriage and is included in bridal bouquets as a fertility charm. Bridesmaids used to plant a sprig of myrtle from the bride's bouquet to see if the cutting grew – if it did, another wedding was promised. In Germany, until the 19th century, it was traditional for the bridesmaids to buy the bride's myrtle wreath. A sprig of myrtle from Queen Victoria's wedding bouquet (1840) was planted at Osborne, Isle of Wight, and thrived. A piece from the bush was included as 'something old' in Princess Anne's bridal bouquet in 1973.

Other perennial favourites include **white lilies**, which symbolise virginity, as do **white roses** – and everyone knows that the **rose** is the flower of love. **Vervain** (fertility, luck and remembrance) is also popular. For constancy, a bride might choose **marigolds**, and if she selects **yarrow** it is said that love will endure for at least seven years.

Orange blossom is a more recent wedding

> **"**
>
> *There's rosemary, that's for remembrance; pray love, remember; and there is pansies, that's for thought.*
>
> William Shakespeare, *Hamlet*
>
> **"**

flower in England, introduced from France in about 1820, though the blossom and the fruit have long been associated with love and marriage in countries where the tree grows naturally. The orange is a symbol of the hope of fruitfulness, therefore it represents fertility, and the white blossom is symbolic of innocence.

Across the Channel, French brides traditionally choose **mignonette** ('little darling') to maintain their husbands' affection. **Lily-of-the-valley** is another French favourite – a traditional May Day love gift.

Japonica or **quince** flowers are symbolic of their fruit which, according to the Ancient Greeks, should be shared to promote marital love.

LOVE TOKENS

Lovers have always enjoyed lavishing gifts on each other. Today, it's flowers, chocolates, toys and underwear, but years ago an ardent lover may have presented the object of his desires with a plaited **straw favour** or a **true lover's knot** (a double knot with two interlacing bows). In Wales in particular, **love spoons**, elaborately carved by a lover for his sweetheart, were very popular. Carved spoons were favourite tokens in other countries, too, and ordinary household spoons played a part in local superstitions. For example, a sure sign of a future wedding was when two teaspoons were accidentally placed on the same saucer, although some said that this was a sign that a girl would marry twice.

It is, of course, very unlucky to lose or break a love token, be it a carved spoon or something more practical like a carved butter-print or a knitting-needle pouch (once a great favourite because the girl would wear it at her waist so that

The huge diamond that Richard Burton gave Elizabeth Taylor as a love 'token' cost him more than a million dollars.

her lover was close to her). The love affair is sure to end badly after such carelessness.

The **love-lock** was high fashion in the 16th century. It was a small curl of hair fastened to the temple rather like the kiss-curls against the cheeks of girls in the early 1960s. It was also known as a 'bow-catcher' – a pun on the word 'beau' (lover). A man's love-curl was jokingly known as a 'bell-rope' (for pulling 'belles', the feminine equivalent of beaux).

LOVE BY ANY OTHER NAME

LOVER: suitor, admirer, follower, adorer, wooer, amoret, bean, sweetheart, inamorato, swain, young man, flame, love, truelove, leman, Lothario, gallant, paramour, amoroso, cavaliere servente, captive, cicisbeo, caro sposo, lady love, idol, darling, duck, Dulcinea, angel, goddess, betrothed, affianced, fiancée, flirt, coquette, amorette, dear, precious, darling, pet, beloved, little, favourite, minion, cosset, idol, jewel, fondling, apple, honey, sweetie pie, mopsey, moppet, sweet, baby, sugar, chick, pigsnie, joy.

COURTSHIP: wooing, suit, addresses, the soft impeachment, serenading, caterwauling, bill-and-coo, spoon, toy, dally, gallivant, philander, make love, ogle, cast sheep's eyes upon, faire les yeux doux.

MATCH: betrothment, nuptials, espousals, epithalamium, Hymen, wedding, bridal, nubile, schatchen.

MARRIAGE: matrimony, wedlock, union, miscegenation, vinculum matrimony, nuptial tie, married state, coverture, bed, cohabitation, Darby and Joan.

PARTNER: spouse, mate, yokemate, feme, feme covert, squaw, lady, wife, helpmate, rib, better half, trouble and strife, grey mare, old Dutch, old woman, old man, husband, man, consort, baron, Benedict, Turk, Bluebeard, levirate, Mormonism, neogamist, live-in lover, beau, mistress, concubine, wife-in-water-colours, guidman and guidwife.

LOVE IN ANY LANGUAGE

English:	Love	Marriage	Wedding	I love you
French:	amour	mariage	noces	Je t'aime
German:	Liebe	Ehe	Hochzeit	Ich liebe Dich
Greek:	agape	pantreia	gamos	Agapo
Italian:	amore	matrimonio	matrimonio	Ti amo
Portuguese:	amor	casamento	casamento	Eu amo-te
Spanish:	amor	matrimonio	boda	Te quiero
Russian:	lyoobov	vrak	svadba	Ja liublu vass
Serbo-Croat:	ljubav	zenidba	vjencanje	Volim te
Afrikaans:	liefde	huwelik	bruilof	Ek het jou lief

English:	Bride	Bridegroom	Bridesmaid	Mother-in-law
French:	épousée	époux	amie de noce	belle-mère
German:	Braut	Bräutigam	Brautjungfer	Schwiegermutter
Greek:	nymphi	gambros	paranymphi	pethera
Italian:	sposa	sposo	damigella d'onore	suocera
Portuguese:	noiva	noivo	dama de honor	sogra
Spanish:	novia	novio	dama de honor	suegra
Russian:	nyevyesta	zhenech	padruzhka	tyoshcha/svyekrov
Serbo-Croat:	mlada	mladozenja	djeverusa	svekrva/punica
Afrikaans:	bruid	bruidegom	strooimeisie	skoonmoeder

The word 'bridegroom' originates from the Old Teutonic word for man – *gumon*, rather than the medieval English word 'groom' meaning manservant.

KEEPING IT IN THE FAMILY

In some cultures, particularly the Islamic, marriage between **cousins** is strongly encouraged. After all, the families already know each other and it is a way of keeping wealth within the extended family. Ideally a girl marries her father's brother's son; likewise a man marries his father's brother's daughter or, failing that, his father's sister's daughter or his mother's brother's daughter. However, marrying closer relatives is not permitted – parents cannot marry their children or stepchildren, just as siblings cannot marry each other. Marrying a niece or nephew is also prohibited. Interestingly, a woman who has suckled a child not her own is deemed to be the same as its natural mother and her relatives are therefore the child's blood relatives. There are also rules preventing Muslims from marrying their in-laws. A married man is allowed to have several wives, but may not marry a wife's sister or aunt unless he has already terminated his marriage to that wife. He cannot marry a woman already living with her husband, nor a prostitute, nor a non-Muslim other than a Jew or Christian. Any Christian or Jewish woman marrying a Muslim is required to sign a statement saying she will bring up the children in the Islamic faith.

In parts of **Central Africa** there are strong taboos against marrying relatives by blood or marriage. For example, a man should not marry his mother-in-law, his wife's mother's sister, his wife's grandmother or sister, his wife's brother's wife, his sister's daughter, his son's wife or his niece's son's wife. In **Malawi** a woman should not marry any of her mother-in-law's uncles.

A man of the Bantu-speaking **Ngombe**, who live in the swampy forests on either side of the Congo river, can inherit his older brother's widows but must never marry a widow of his younger brother. The senior son sometimes inherits his father's widows.

Among the **Ahafo Ashanti** and the **Agni** tribes in West Africa, it is considered best to marry a cross-cousin but incestuous to marry someone with the same matrilineal ancestor. The **Fanti** of southern Ghana have a matrilineal society but consider marriage between a couple with the same 'father's deity' (ie descended from common patrilineal ancestry) to be incestuous.

There is a strict caste system among many of the **Indian** tribes along the north-west coast of North America. It is forbidden to marry someone in the

The Papago and Pima Indians of south-west USA and north Sonora have a complicated extended family system with special names for each relationship, and it is further complicated by marriage. Love is *pihk elidaDag* or *si tatchua*; to marry off is *hohnchud*. A man's wife is *ni-hohnig* and he is her *kun*, but informally he calls her *ni-oksga* and she calls him *ni-kehliga*. Let Dean and Lucille Saxton, who compiled a Papago-Pima dictionary in 1969, explain:

'The terms for in-laws are made by extension through the child. My father's sihs (older brother, sister or cousin) who calls me *ni-chuhchuD* calls my mother *ni-chuchuD-je'e*. My father's shehpij (younger brother, sister or cousin) who calls me *ni-hakimaD* calls my mother *ni-hamima-je'e*. My mother's sihs who calls me *ni-maD* calls my father *ni-maD-ohg*. My mother's shehpij who calls me *ni-ma'i* calls my father *ni-ma'i-ohg*. My father's father's side and generation who call me *ni-wosmaD* call my mother *ni-wosma-je'e*. My father's mother's side and generation who call me *ni-ka'amaD* call my mother *ni-ka'ama-je'e*. My mother's father's side and generation who call me *ni-ba'amaD* call my father *ni-ba'amaD-ohg*. My mother's mother's side and generation who call me *ni-mohs* call my father *ni-mohs-ohg*. Each of these reciprocate with exactly the same term so that my mother also calls one of my father's father's side and generation *ni-wosma-je'e*, etc. I would call my stepfather *ni-hakit* and he would . . .' and so it goes on. Second marriages make it all even more complicated!

In the Solomon Islands, boys too young to marry wore special bulbous grass hats to warn off the girls, who were not supposed to flirt with them.

same clan and a man takes his clanship from his mother's side, not his father's, with the result that each father belongs to a different clan from his children. There is a common custom of a man marrying the daughter of a maternal uncle, if he can work out what the clan relationship is!

In the widespread **Baha'i** faith, marriage between kinsfolk is initially referred to the spiritual assemblies of the Universal House of Justice. Without exception, a man cannot marry his stepmother, but he can remarry a wife he has already divorced.

MIX AND MATCH

The **Roman Catholic Church** in England and Wales recently relaxed its regulations slightly regarding mixed marriages, though a couple must still raise their children as Catholics. The Church introduced a revised form of the promise required of a prospective Catholic marriage partner to obtain consent to marry a non-Catholic. But the promise no longer has to be in writing, nor does the other partner have to consent to it, although he or she should be made fully aware of it. A new phrase –'within the unity of our partnership' – has been inserted and some interpret this as meaning that the Catholic partner should not so press insistence on their children's Catholic upbringing that the marriage is jeopardised.

A **Masai** warrior in Uganda was not allowed to marry at all during his service as a warrior – he lived in barracks with other warriors. Indeed, in

A Hungarian boy of the Matyo tribe (near Miskole in the north) can only marry a girl who lives in the same village street. Also, it is considered improper for a man of the Matyo to show any affection towards his fiancée or his wife!

the **British Army** it was a tradition that men could only marry if they were at least 26 years old and had five years' service; even then their future wives were surreptitiously vetted for suitability. The 19th-century term 'married crocks' referred to men and women married with the approval of the regiment.

The **Wolof** tribe of Senegal and Gambia are predominantly Muslim and traditionally cultivators, with a complex system of co-operative working groups and a rigid social hierarchy. The top social level is made up of those of 'freeborn'

Seretse Khama was no ordinary law student – when he came to London he was heir to the chieftainship of the ruling tribe of Bechuanaland (now Botswana). In 1947 he fell in love with Ruth Williams, but when they became engaged a year later, both their families were furious at the match. Her parents were probably colour prejudiced, but in Bechuanaland the problem was more substantial. If the people refused to accept the foreign white bride, it was possible that the tribe might break up and British rule in the protectorate would have been jeopardised. Also, the Union of South Africa was at the time beginning to institutionalise apartheid and Attlee's Government in Britain feared that such an important mixed marriage right on South Africa's doorstep would encourage her to pull out of the Commonwealth and annex Bechuanaland. The British Government failed both in stopping the lovers' marriage and in forcing Seretse to abdicate, but the couple were banished from his homeland indefinitely. Fortunately the marriage was a strong one and survived intact, with Seretse eventually being elected as the first prime minister of Bechuanaland in 1965 and as president of the new Botswana the following year, having become Sir Seretse. He was re-elected several times in succession and died in 1980. Not only was Lady Khama accepted by her husband's nation but she is still respected and honoured there. Love conquers all!

Transsexual model Caroline Cossey, also known as Tula, was born biologically a boy and christened Barry in 1955. Always psychologically effeminate, he changed his name to Caroline by deed poll in 1973, and began a course of hormone tablets, followed by breast implants and a final operation (at the age of 20) to complete his physical sex change to become a 'she'. In 1976, she was issued a UK passport as a woman and became a model. She is now a woman in all respects except chromosomally – and except in the eyes of British law concerning marriage.

In 1984, she became engaged but failed to convince the British authorities to re-issue her with a birth certificate as a female, or to allow her to marry her Italian fiancé. She took her case to the European Commission on Human Rights, but when the case was heard in Strasbourg in 1990, she lost her case against the British government – legally she is still male and therefore has no right to marry another man. Her chromosomes were deemed to be more defining than her profound sense of femininity in all other respects – emotional, psychological and physical. However, not all European countries are so 'rigid' in their 'scientific' laws.

In 1970, the marriage of transsexual model April Ashley (formerly a merchant seaman) to Arthur Corbett was annulled after a High Court action. They had married in Gibraltar.

In November 1990, a 'marriage' between two men was annulled in a London divorce court on the grounds that both parties were male. Ian Franklin, a horologist, had gone through a registry office ceremony in Brent, London, with Harley Jones (born Robert Duxbury) in 1985, without revealing that Jones had been born a man and had undergone a sex change operation in 1981. Jones did not contest the annulment.

Transsexual model Caroline Cossey (Tula) who was born biologically male. In 1990, she was refused permission to marry her fiancé.

descent, then come the blacksmiths and leather workers (the only two groups which can inter-marry), followed by the 'slaves', the minstrels and, lastly, the slaves of the minstrels. Relatives in the same patrilineage (tracing as far back as the great-great-grandfather) cannot marry, and anyone wishing to get married must first consult the elder of his patrilineal kinship group about his choice of partner.

TASKS AND TRIALS

The path of true love is not supposed to be easy. Even if the hurdle of winning the affection of the beloved can be overcome, society seeks to impose its own hurdles before the couple can be joined in marriage – emphasising the importance of this major step in life.

It was ever thus. Mythology reflects reality, albeit distorted by magnification. For example, all sorts of impossible tasks would be set, usually imposed by the girl's father on her hopeful lover. The essence of the impediments which obstruct him is not so much the physical climbing of moun-tains and slaying of unlikely beasts and giants as the proving of his worth in the eyes of his future father-in-law. Today there are more subtle ways of achieving such acceptance than by dealing with dragons and witches – but there will always be obstacles! In a way, they serve to test the earnest-ness of the suitor – does he really want to make an honest woman of the girl or is he simply playing with her affections?

The Celtic story of **Kulhwch** and **Olwen** is typical of the genre. To make the tale more realis-tic, try to imagine people you know in the starring roles . . .

Olwen was the beautiful, innocent daughter of a giant who set Kulhwch, who was in love with her, 13 tasks, all connected with preparations for the wedding feast. These included clearing and culti-vating some thicket-covered ground to produce meat, drink and flax (to make linen for the bride's veil); finding special sweet honey and stealing a magic cup, pouring horn, cornucopian hamper, cooking cauldron and harp from various terrifying monsters and warriors. He also had to deal with ferocious wild boars and use their tusks as tools to dress the giant's beard and hair (with the help of a witch's blood) so that he looked his best. There were also 26 subsidiary tasks and the whole ven-ture involved travelling through strange lands (with the unexpected help of various guides along the way – mostly women or animals) to meet Olwen, followed by the completion of the tasks (again, with unexpected help – from ants, super-naturals, old animals and even King Arthur him-self) in hostile territory. In the end, Kulhwch had to slaughter the giant to bridge the gap between Olwen and himself, and he succeeded in winning her as his bride.

The theme of this story, with its familiar ele-ments of the unobtainable maiden, the journey across strange lands, the series of tasks (often riddles rather than physical acts), the overcoming of the father and the elopement with the bride, would be recognised worldwide. It epitomises courtship – and you thought *you* had problems?

Shakespeare was more down to earth. **Portia**, the eligible heiress in *The Merchant of Venice*, had plenty of suitors and their task was to choose one of three caskets. The silver one was inscribed, 'Who chooseth me shall get as much as he deserves' – which seems as good a comment as any on the gamble of marriage!

2
Caught!

MATCHMAKING

'Marriages are made in heaven,' some say, but matchmaking is done on earth. Modern lovers are just as superstitious as ever, but instead of depending on apple parings and lucky leaves, or love charms and Cupid's haphazard arrows, they trust to the oracles of our times – computers, television and advertising.

Meeting the high demand for compatible partners in a mobile society such as ours is a thriving section of the national economy. With an ever-increasing number of people moving to unfamiliar towns in the course of their work, and with more and more finding less time to socialise, many face loneliness. Indeed, the modern matchmakers now form quite an important social 'welfare' industry.

Dateline, established in Britain in 1966, claims to be the world's largest computer-dating agency with more than 35 000 members in this country and more than 3000 new clients each month. The company uses an in-house computer to match suitable people, mainly with the aim of producing long-term relationships, many of which eventually lead to marriage.

Not all the applicants can be satisfied, however. The most difficult to suit are those who live in rural areas (because of the problems of travelling to meet each other) or fall within 'difficult' age ranges. For example, in this country there are three times as many single women over 50 as single men, and about twice as many eligible young men under 25 as young women.

Those who join Dateline range in age from 17 to 70 – the majority are single and aged 35 or less, and are mostly of European origin. More women than men have been married before, while just under a third of the clients are graduates, but 15% have no educational qualifications at all. Of the total membership 68% do not smoke and 41% do not want to meet someone who smokes. Dateline's questionnaire, completed by new clients when they join the service, runs to nearly 200 questions.

The British also use the services of more exclusive marriage bureaux, such as that of **Heather Jenner**, or several others which are advertised in papers like *The Times*, whose readers are expected to be successful high-flying careerists or extremely cultured!

In Moscow, where weddings can seem like factory production lines (a continual stream of brides in identical white dresses and veils queuing up

In Singapore, premier Lee Kuan Yew encouraged the use of a Japanese computer programme to matchmake for female graduates in particular. He had been alarmed to discover that uneducated women were producing twice as many children as the educated and he feared that the national level of intelligence (and hence the economy) would deteriorate.

before the Soviet Registrar), some women are now looking hopefully towards Britain for their husbands through a new matchmaking bureau, the **Moscow Connection**. This advertises its services on Soviet television and invites women to look for husbands in 'dear old England'. The women must be under 40 years old, able to speak some English, reasonably attractive and with no serious illness. About 1000 British men have already registered but the girls might be sadly disappointed – their image of an Englishman is halfway between Sherlock Holmes and Prince Charles, and they anticipate old-world courtesy!

Indeed dating agencies and marriage bureaux are springing up all over the Soviet Union now, especially in Moscow. The official dating agency there is known as **Blitz** because of its 'blitz evenings' during which groups of 30 people are allowed just enough time to give each other the once-over, swap telephone numbers and, with luck, depart with a possible partner. Each group of 15 men (aged between 50 and 60) and 15 women (from 45 to 50) is assembled by age, height, education and skills in a crude attempt to better the chances of compatibility. The women are settled into cosy armchairs while the men perch opposite them on a row of less comfortable seats for precisely three minutes of chat. Then a bell rings and the men all move one place to the left. Forty-five minutes later each man has sat opposite each woman and their assessments have been made. The agency also offers 'cosy evenings', an astrology service for the starry-eyed and a 3000-card index with photographs through which clients can browse.

The **Alliance** marriage bureau is more classy. Clients are received like guests by well-dressed women in a splendid hall where they meet the private organisation's founder, Ms Tamara Alekseyeva, for a personal interview. She adds their details to her card index and helps them to devise small-ads for her in-house journal. A single advertisement by one Viktor produced more than 1600 replies: he responded to only one of them, proposed to its writer two months later and is now married to her. Alliance has already helped about 1000 couples into marriage.

Most of those who apply to these dating agencies and marriage bureaux are women. As Ms

Right: Civil wedding in USSR, c. 1920, under the Red Flag.

Below: Marriage by mutual agreement in China.

Alekseyeva remarked to *Guardian* features writer Dana Schmidt in January, 1991: 'Women find it harder to go off hunting for a man, but easier to imagine that they're having a bad time without one and that they're not in a position to find a new partner.'

In London, Laila El-Essawy started her **Islamic 'Matchmaker'** marriage bureau in 1988, in response to the growing needs of a traditional Muslim community trying to come to terms with the British way of life. Most Asian marriages in Britain are still arranged, but it is often a problem for those living in this country to find suitable partners. By 1990, Matchmaker had about 200 Muslims on its books, ranging from hotel receptionists to millionaires. Only the men are charged a fee, paying £100 on registration and a further £500 for a successfully arranged marriage. There are roughly equal numbers of applications from men and women.

In Hackney, London, the local **Pakistan Women's Welfare Centre** acts as an unpaid matchmaker for Asians by introducing suitably matched families. It also acts as a go-between for young couples who have already chosen each other but are unwilling to tell their parents, perhaps because an arranged partner is already standing by in Pakistan. If matters between parents and children come to an impasse, the Centre contacts as many relatives as possible in an attempt to resolve the young couple's problem.

Matchmaking is an ancient tradition in China, but it has now been brought up to date. Every Friday and Saturday there are television dating programmes carrying advertisements for mates and there are public parks where singles meet and compare age, work and education. There are matchmaking officers in every city district, and now there is the **Great Wall of Information**, set up in May 1989, with its brand-new Computer Matchmaker. The Chinese seek *choice* – girls are bored with meeting men only at work, where they have too much in common, for example. Women are considered to be on the shelf at more than 25 years old and they, along with divorcees, are looking for husbands with university degrees, two to ten years older than themselves, and at least 5ft 5in (1.6m) tall. ('Short male workers are the most difficult to place,' says GWI's vice-president, Xu

Fengshan.) Men want beautiful women at least two to five years younger than themselves, and are intimidated by a good education. For only 20 yuan (about £2.20) registrants are offered a minimum of ten compatible strangers. About 600 people sign on every month; two-thirds are men and, of those in their 30s, a third have been divorced. Out of the 4000 people who registered between December 1989 and September 1990, 30 couples have married.

The use of **video** gives computer-dating an extra dimension, for better or for worse, and it at least improves the chances of matching suitable couples who have something more in common than a completed questionnaire.

Cilla Black's well-known and long-running television matchmaker, **Blind Date**, is much more of a lottery. The participating 'chooser' fires three questions (usually insubstantial) at the potential dates, who remain hidden behind a screen, and the choice is made based on their answers. Then comes the appalling embarrassment as the chosen one emerges. As if to add insult to injury, the couple are requested to return to the programme following their 'date' – usually to confess that it was a disaster!

All this is tame, though, when compared to Japanese television matchmaking programmes. The couples sometimes go through far more rigorous and self-ridiculing procedures during the mutual selection process, and they are alarmingly frank in their public assessment of each other.

Many Japanese marriages are arranged through a **nakado** or professional matchmaker, and about half the nation's marriages are still arranged with the help of a go-between of some kind – if not a nakado or marriage bureau, then a family go-between, a teacher or even an employer.

The West African **Wolof** tribe have a social system which includes several working co-operatives divided into different groups for the various stages of life. The Wolofs love parties and often a young unmarried women's group will visit other villages to ask young men for gifts. Back in their own village the women repay them by holding parties lasting for several days. This gives everyone an opportunity to meet potential marriage partners, though in theory marriages are arranged by parents.

A women's working group has several roles to play during courtship and at the wedding. The suitor must give the group a large bundle of kola nuts as a public announcement of the couple's engagement (after which his betrothed may not receive any other male visitors) and the group later helps to prepare the wedding celebrations, and accompanies the bride to her new home.

LONELY HEARTS

Advertising for a mate is nothing new. Even in the 18th century, some American newspapers had columns of lonely-heart advertisements in which individuals clearly stated their attributes almost as explicitly as they might today, and certainly as wittily. Here are some modern examples:

Mona Lisa in her prime. Soft, dark hair and figure fine. She loves music, books and laughter. A kindly man is what she's after.

London male, 36, single, solvent, sincere, sensible, strong, sensitive, slim, sporty, smokeless; seeks shortish, size sixteen soulmate.

African prince, next in line to a throne, also a chartered engineer, London/Essex based, tall, dark, handsome, sporty, rich, caring and loving, 29. Wishes to hear from tall, upmarket, blonde English lady, 20–30yrs, to share privileges of royalty with. Nonsmoker. Anywhere in Britain.

Large lady sought by thinking Manchester male, 40, 6ft, 12½ stone, honest, affectionate, good humoured; into home life, classical music, jazz, art. Seeks tidy, easygoing, spontaneous, caring partner.

An outstanding Chinese, single, 30, 5ft 11in, medium built, and smart looking (no glasses), very well educated with top British business qualifications, cultured, sincere, open minded and affectionate personality, with humour, ambitions, many interests, and other good qualities. Seeks a sincere, feminine, pretty and single lady, under 32, who wants to have a life of lasting love, care and cultural diversity.

Slightly imperfect! Widower, built 1946, slim, 5ft 10in; seeks caring owner, 35–45, to share future.

Through the mists of an early morn a tall, blond and devastatingly attractive Knight rides. His intelligence and wit contradict his strong muscular frame and 23 years of age. He seeks a fair maiden of similar characteristics . . . This Knight may be bold, but lonely.

Wanting attractive, petite, quality woman, with high morals and virginity. Should be reasonably intelligent and of middle class upbringing, sincerity and down-to-earth personality vital, nonsmoker, and fair-skinned.

Can I pollute your airspace? Still smoking at 51, still attractive, slim, blue eyes, brown hair (with help), great sense of humour and personality. Now that I'm out of hibernation, divorced, working in caring profession, own home, own car, will someone please find me? Knight in shining armour would do nicely thank you.

Berks – but prefers to purr. Divorced, with ten year old, I am 43, blue eyed, willowy, and have a sunny, affectionate nature . . .

Lively, attractive, slim but cuddly, ice-cream making ex-teacher, seeks light-hearted wooer of pinkish green sensibilities.

Bath based swan, cygnets flown; seeks gentleman companion, to fill this empty place in my heart.

Reformed M.C.P. seeks young replacement girlfriend as current paramour, although loyal and faithful for past several years, is now getting on a bit and no longer looks her best. No abusive replies, sense of humour essential.

In 1990, a farmer's wife advertised her four single daughters in the personal column of *Farmers' Weekly*: 'Man-eating daughters of Zelophehad seek strong partners for life-safari.' The girls became quite famous when the national press seized on the story.

FARM CHARM

In 1989, a survey of farm daughters, covering those aged 18 to 40, revealed that 38.5% were unmarried, 28.7% were married to farmers and the rest to non-farmers; 64% still lived in rural areas and, of those who did not, 64% wanted to! But there are considerable problems of loneliness in the British countryside today and farming families are increasingly seeking help from marriage guidance counsellors and the Samaritans.

Farmer's wife **Patricia Warren** has set up a special marriage bureau to meet the needs of lonely landsmen. Her clients range from crofters and hill farmers to East Anglian grain barons.

Farming is the main occupation in the Lisdoonvarna region of County Clare in Ireland, where local hotelier Jim White arranges an annual **Festival of the Bachelors** each September. By

In St Petersburg, Russia, an annual bride parade was held each Whit Monday in the 19th century. Potential brides were displayed with their wealth and other attributes, and a week later the serious business of arranging marriages began.

local tradition people marry late and many of the local bachelors tend to be well past youth and not at all at ease socially. Sometimes Mr White has to 'import' parties of potential partners – he once brought in a plane-load of American matrons from Chicago but the experiment was not a huge success.

In Ancient Greece, Sparta (in the south-east Peloponnese) was an extraordinary place with a perhaps unique society. The sole business of a Spartan citizen was war and all men were trained to it from birth, with a strong emphasis on physical fitness, discipline, and indifference to pain. Unlike the highly respectable women in the rest of Greece, Spartan girls had the same physical training as the boys – and they all practised their gymnastics together completely naked. According to Plutarch, the Greek philosopher, the aim was that 'the maidens should harden their bodies with exercise of running, wrestling, throwing the bar, and casting the dart, to the end that the fruit wherewith they might be afterwards conceived, taking nourishment of a strong and lusty body, should shoot out and spread the better' and they would more readily bear the pains of childbirth. 'And though the maidens did show themselves thus naked openly, yet was there no dishonesty seen nor offered,' though Plutarch said that those naked plays, sports and dances were 'provocations to draw and allure the young men to marry: not as persuaded by

geometrical reasons, as saith Plato, but brought to it by liking, and of very love.'

Once over the age of 20, any Spartan could marry, but even married men had to live in 'men's houses' until they were 30, and had to conduct their marriages as if they were illicit affairs. This custom, it was claimed, greatly enhanced the marriage by keeping love exciting and alive. However, the main point of marriage was to produce more soldiers and so a childless wife was quite happy to obey the state's orders to find a more potent partner than her husband, especially if he was much older than she, and no dishonour accrued to him if she did so. Incidentally, Aristotle, an earlier Greek philosopher, claimed that Spartan women were dominant, mischievous, decadent and quite ungovernable!

Spartan men who did not marry were ridiculed and forced to parade naked outside the places where the young exercised and danced. However, homosexual love between men was an accepted custom, and was even thought to have an educational role – a boy had to be a credit to his lover, who could be fined for the boy's lack of bravery in his war training.

Aristotle, the Ancient Greek philosopher, thought that everybody should be loved in proportion to their worth and that, ergo, wives should love their husbands more because men were superior. However, men were supposed to recognise women's dominance in their own spheres, including their knowledge that children should never be conceived when the wind was blowing from the north! Couples were not to marry too young because their children would be weak and female, the wife would be wanton and the husband's growth would be stunted! Women had to wait until they were 18, and men 37.

In Plato's Utopia (his imaginary 'perfect' society) no man could have his own wife. In order to keep the population figures constant, boys and girls would be brought together at certain festivals by drawing lots – or so they believed. In fact, the elders ensured that the best 'sires' would have the most opportunity for fathering children. The children were removed at birth so that no one could identify their parents. Fathers were aged between 25 and 55, mothers between 20 and 40; outside those ages intercourse was freely allowed but any child of the union had to be aborted or killed at birth. Men and women had absolute equality in all things.

In Sir Thomas More's *Utopia* (1516), life for the most part was overwhelmingly boring in its lack of individuality, but a bride and groom were actively encouraged to see each other naked before the wedding so that they knew exactly what they were getting!

ARRANGED MARRIAGES

Arranged marriages are customary among Asian **Hindus**. Every opportunity is taken to 'look over' other people's unmarried young at the elaborate and lengthy wedding ceremonies. Afterwards, the girl's parents usually make the initial approach, perhaps by letter or through a friend, and the boy's parents respond by inviting the girl and her parents to their home. They use formal questioning to discover more about her and the extent of her education and, if both sets of parents and the couple themselves approve, another meeting takes place to negotiate the dowry and plan the ceremony. Nowadays, dowries are illegal but gifts are generally given. Girls are not allowed to have boyfriends, let alone have sex before marriage, but sex within the marriage is considered to be a sacred duty. For a long time, public acknowledgement of an 'alliance' was enough to ratify a Hindu marriage, whether arranged or voluntary, and – particularly in India – marriage is for life.

In the **Islamic** religion, any sexual relationship outside marriage is utterly condemned. Muslim couples are not allowed unchaperoned meetings before marriage, but every effort is made to let them get to know each other through family and social gatherings, so that the pair can be sure of a good basis for mutual understanding. It is the duty of the girl and her family to be satisfied that she and her proposed partner have adequate common ground. It is preferable that there are similarities in education, family background, age and, above all, high morality. The wishes of the couple are taken into account even if the marriage was originally arranged by the family so, it follows that, if either party was forced into it, the marriage contract can be invalidated. Either partner can subsequently divorce, but only if there is severe incompatibility. Legally, a man can have up to four wives.

Socrates (according to his pupil, Plato) said that a philosopher should not care for the pleasures of love; his concern was supposed to be with the soul, not the body. However, he should marry and beget children as long as he did so 'absentmindedly'.

A Brahmin wedding in India, c. 1870. Rituals involving fire were central to the ceremony.

Among **Sikhs**, parents have a duty to arrange, and contribute actively towards, their child's marriage. Sometimes the couple will not have met before the nuptials, though in more recent years this has become less common and their agreement to the marriage will have been sought. Before the actual ceremony, which is elaborate, there might be a formal betrothal ceremony at the boy's home, or a more binding one in a Sikh temple.

In **Buddhism**, there are no arranged marriages but the parents' wishes are important. Betrothal is not a private or casual affair – it is the joining of two family groups. It is said that the highest profit a man can gain on earth is a good wife, and the choice of partner is based on love with a responsi-

Charles Darwin drew up a balance sheet when thinking about the possibility of marriage, setting good points and bad points in separate lists. He finally decided that the balance was in favour of the married state. He already had a bride in mind, and he married her a year later.

William Cobbett, a man who cared passionately about the lot of agricultural workers and rural villagers, advised young men to look for eight major qualities in a possible wife: chastity, sobriety, industry, frugality, cleanliness, domesticity, good temper and, finally, beauty. He did not mention love!

bility to each other's families. Marriage is regarded as an alliance in which each partner works to fulfil the aims of the partnership.

For those in societies where arranged marriages are not the norm and it is all, more or less, a matter of **free choice**, there is the agony of having to make one's own decision about the suitability of a future spouse. Some people carefully weigh up the pros and cons as relentlessly as any matchmaking computer, checking compatibility factors and calculating the advantages and disadvantages of the married state. For the great majority, however, it is a matter where heart overrules head, regardless of past experience, whether it is a first marriage or yet another in a succession. We never learn!

A traditional Buddhist marriage in a temple at Seoul, Korea, in 1986.

THE PRICE IS RIGHT

Stripped of electronics, the modern marriage bureau is simply continuing the ancient tradition of matchmaking, though perhaps with rather different criteria to those of old. For centuries, love and marriage were separate, and the bride did not necessarily have any choice in the matter at all – she married whichever man her parents, extended family or tribal group thought suitable, and the choice was generally based on practical considerations such as status and material wealth. 'Love' was an emotional sideline indulged in with extramarital partners, sometimes frowned upon but often widely accepted or even encouraged. In more primitive times, brides were property – they could be captured, exchanged, bought and so on, and many of our own wedding customs hark back to such procedures.

In Anglo-Saxon times, prospective husbands paid their brides' fathers a negotiated price – not to buy the bride but to compensate the father for the loss of his daughter's services. Such a

A betrothal ceremony in the 15th century – the scene here is probably a handfast espousal. But who is incarcerated in the tower? It looks like the bride's disapproving father!

brideprice or bridewealth is still common in African agricultural communities where a woman's labour is of value. This is in contrast to the traditional dowry, which is a lump sum (or goods in kind) which the woman brings into the marriage. It is usually supplied by the father or, failing him, her brothers or, among some tribes, her uncle, though in other cultures girls work to raise their own dowries. Sometimes the dowry is the girl's weight in gold and silver coins, so presumably, the heavier the better!

Although it was not a formal custom, 50 years ago, women among the Goajiro Indians in Colombia were sometimes sold to the rich merchants of Rio Hacha, and it was their maternal uncles who arranged the terms of the deal. Men were allowed as many wives as they could purchase and support.

In medieval Europe, the marriages of the nobility were arranged for three main purposes: to preserve and increase the family wealth, to ally to an equally or more important family, and to ensure the continuation of the family's male line. Occasionally, the son of a high family would marry the daughter of a rich bourgeois, or one of the lesser nobility, to bring greater wealth into his family, but a daughter was never allowed to marry beneath herself socially. Often the bride and groom would not meet until the dowry had been settled and all the arrangements made for the marriage. If the family coffers were insufficient for a daughter's dowry, she remained a spinster at home or disappeared into a nunnery.

A morganatic marriage was a 17th- or 18th-century marriage between a man of high rank (usually royal) and a woman of lower social standing. She was not allowed to acquire his rank, nor could she or any of the children of the marriage be entitled to inherit the title or possessions. The name comes from the Latin word morganatica meaning a groom's gift to his bride, and morgengabe was the Old High German for the 'morning-gift' from the husband to the wife after the consummation of such a marriage. The gift was the only claim to her husband's possessions that she could make. Morganatic marriages were also called 'left-handed marriages' because the husband would pledge his troth with his left hand rather than his right.

In medieval Wales and Ireland, the most sought-after marriages were by gift of kin (a contract made between consenting families for partners of comparable status, with plenty of bargaining beforehand about the dowry and the brideprice). The economics and respectability of the match were all-important and there was no need for mutual attraction between the couple. This was deemed to be 'real life', in complete contrast to the typically romantic Celtic myths of elopement and abduction. In real life treasure was wealth and status rather than love.

Among the Wolof tribe in Africa, the bride-wealth is high and the cost of a wedding expensive because of all the feasting, so men tend not to marry until they are at least 25. In the 1940s the bridewealth was equal to at least a year's average income, but the couple's co-operative working groups always contributed to the costs (for the first marriage only) by donating money, grain, livestock and kola nuts.

In parts of West Africa, the payment of bridewealth is now more of a token to guarantee the stability of the marriage (it is often refundable if the marriage breaks down). More important is a new courtship payment offered to the girl's family as a token of the man's serious intent in the early stages of the courtship, though it is nominal in value. Increasingly the young are initiating their own courtship and marriage, without first consulting their parents, but they still desire family approval of their choice. Traditionally many marry people from the same village or a neighbouring one, but with more mobile populations and workforces many others are marrying away from the home villages.

The increasing economic independence of African women has led to a growth in the number of 'soma' marriages (ie with no payment of bridewealth at all). In some areas women even own their farms and can hire labourers – they no

The Bolivian tin millionaire, Don Simon Iturbi Patino (1861-1947), paid a dowry of £8 million on behalf of his daughter Elena in 1929 – a record which still stands.

The origin of the word 'bachelor' is disputed. Some say it is based on the Latin word *vacca* (a cow) and meant a cowherd or farmworker. Later it became the word for a young man who aspired to become a knight, and eventually it was the name for a university graduate (hence the French *baccalauréat*).

The origin of the word 'spinster' comes from the belief that the ability to spin wool and flax was an essential attribute in a wife – a girl was not considered marriage-worthy until she had spun enough to create her own trousseau. Thus a spinster was a girl who was still desperately trying to spin enough to fill her bride-box.

longer need to marry for material security. And men, too, can hire farm labour, so are less in need of a wife's work on the farm.

In south-east Nigeria, the **Afikpo Ibo** men might still pay brideprice even if the couple are Christians and well educated. Indeed, in the 1970s in urban areas, there was a dramatic inflation in the acceptable brideprice, depending on the extent of the bride's formal education. Fathers believed they were entitled to some return on their investment in their daughters' education. This inflation quickly led to a decrease in polygyny, because it was difficult for husbands to raise more than one brideprice, and in contrast there was an increase in later marriages, common-law marriages and prostitution. In addition, it was felt that educated women should not demean their new status by actually working after marriage – and men began to resent paying inflated brideprices for such a useless asset as a wasted education.

The **Anang Ibibiu** tribe of south-east Nigeria consider polygyny to be the ideal, but monogamy has become far more common because the bridewealth is so high. It is refundable on divorce, though some district officials deem that if a woman has already looked after her husband for several years and borne his children, the bridewealth has been cancelled out and no refund is due.

Traditionally, all over Africa, **cattle** essentially represent wealth (four-legged bank accounts, in fact) and are the most important part of a marriage contract. The standard price for an average Zulu bride, for example, is 13 cattle. Among the 'cattle culture' peoples such as the Masai, Fulani, Nuer and Angoni, the bridewealth or *lobola* consists of an exchange of cattle between the families as an act of faith. 'We do not buy brides, only concubines,' said an old Swazi. The cattle are held in trust by the bride's father to ensure that she becomes a good wife. If she disappoints (perhaps by failing to bear children), her husband can demand the return of the entrusted cattle – not just any animals but *his* cattle, which can make life awkward for the father-in-law if he has already disposed of them! Until very recently only native cattle were acceptable for lobola – European imports were considered very inferior. So important was the ownership of large numbers of cattle among such people in the 19th century that they pitied poor Queen Victoria – she had fewer cattle than many of her own subjects and therefore, they reasoned, could not have been a powerful or respected ruler.

In the **Solomon Islands**, brides were purchased by exchanging pigs – from one to 20, depending on the qualities of the bride.

Brides were still being purchased in the **Turkoman Republic** (USSR) 50 years ago, although the practice was forbidden by law.

In **France**, there were sometimes public collections to get a dowry together in rural areas. Groups of pretty girls would give the donors a glass of wine and a kiss in return for their contributions.

Among **Hindus** and **Sikhs**, including those in Britain, the bride's family is often expected to pay a dowry to the husband though India's 1961 Dowry Prohibition Act was designed to end the dowry customs and so reduce the frequent suicides of brides. The legislation does not extend to Britain and some grooms' families still demand cash and gold from the brides' families. If a girl's dowry is considered inadequate, she may find it humiliating

In Hungary, a wealthy bride in the late 1930s needed three carts to carry her trousseau to her new home. It included furniture, three mattresses, three bedcovers, an eiderdown, five embroidered sheets, 18 pillows, 30 shirts, 27 blouses, 18 skirts, four petticoats, 29 scarves, 12 kerchiefs, 16 aprons, and a dress to wear when she baked bread.

No doubt many a woman has 'married a mixen for the sake of the muck' – or married an otherwise undesirable man for the sake of his money.

ENGAGED

The Courtship of the Yonghy-Bonghy-Bo – *Edward Lear's sad story of a rejected suitor.*

'Lady Jingly! Lady Jingly!
        Sitting where the pumpkins blow,
Will you come and be my wife?'
        Said the Yonghy-Bonghy-Bo.
'I am tired of living singly, –
        On this coast so wild and shingly, –
I'm aweary of my life:
        If you'll come and be my wife,
Quite serene would be my life!'
        Said the Yonghy-Bonghy-Bo.'

Edward Lear, *Nonsense Rhymes*

when she lives with her in-laws in the traditional manner, and suicides have been committed. In India itself, official sources published in 1989 said that five Indian women were murdered every day in 'dowry burnings' but the real figure could be ten times as many. The women are doused with kerosene and their saris set alight, but the death is often disguised as a suicide or a kitchen accident.

A bride's **trousseau** was originally her own gift to the marriage, to some extent compensating for the payment of any brideprice. Essentially it consisted of household linen and clothes but in some places a great deal more – mattresses, pillows, furniture, kitchenware and so on (items which today are often given by friends of the couple as wedding presents). The gradual accumulation of a trousseau used to be of great importance to young women in Europe and America and they kept it not in a 'bottom drawer' but in beautifully carved or painted chests and oval bride-boxes.

The value of a **Lithuanian** trousseau is traditionally measured by its wealth of beautiful embroidery.

In **Germany** at the turn of the century, the bride's dowry was carried to her new home in an elaborate cart and included items which symbolised her new responsibilities, usually a spinning wheel, a bed complete with pillows, a chest and a cradle.

There on the coast of Coromandel, the tiny-bodied, moon-faced Yonghy-Bonghy-Bo offered his Lady his worldly goods – two old chairs, half a candle, an old jug without a handle, and all the shrimps, prawns, fish and watercress that his wooded coast could offer. But he was too late, for the Lady already had a fiancé in England, Handel Jones Esquire, who often sent her milk-white Dorking hens. Tearfully, she told her little suitor: 'I can merely be your friend.' Devastated, he fled to the sea, climbed onto the back of a large friendly turtle and disappeared towards the sunset, saying his farewell. His Lady remained at Coromandel, never to leave it, mourning him. Some say that the author of this sad tale, Edward Lear, cast himself in the role of that little man.

"————————————————

I have a view that one should not make the decision to marry unless it is absolutely irresistible. It was.

Literary agent Hilary Rubinstein, after 35 years as the husband of Helge Rubinstein, editor of the *Oxford Book of Marriage*

————————————————————**"**

"————————————————

Congreve wrote of a young woman receiving a proposal. Her reaction was: *'My dear liberty, shall I leave thee? My faithful solitude, my darling contemplation, must I bid you then adieu? Aye, adieu – my morning thoughts, agreeable wakings, indolent slumbers, all ye douceurs, ye sommeils du matin, adieu.'*

————————————————————**"**

'Happy they'll be that wed and wive within **leap year**: they're sure to survive,' refers to the tradition that a woman can propose to a man during a leap year.

Leap years apart, by a 13th-century Scottish law (also upheld in several other countries) a man could be fined for rejecting a woman's proposal, unless he could prove that he was already committed to another. The fine might have been £1, or a silk gown to compensate the rejected girl.

A **Kikuyu** warrior in Kenya would go courting with the tip of his lance sheathed in plumes. If the girl took his lance from him, she accepted him as her husband.

After the fun and games of anticipation and the excitement and heartaches of courtship, the **engagement** (or betrothal) marks the couple's serious intent to marry. The step is often considered as almost as irrevocable as marriage itself, especially when it has been formally announced.

In many cultures the period of engagement is traditionally a long one, with plenty of time for the couple to learn more about each other and to prepare for marriage both practically and emotionally. Quite suddenly, the couple have stepped over an invisible threshold of respectability and maturity – the great 'rite of passage' has begun and from then on they find themselves swept up in a wave of activity that reaches its crescendo at the wedding ceremony.

In the West, many couples – or perhaps their parents – like to announce the engagement formally and publicly, often in the newspapers, so that everybody knows of it and the pressure mounts. Meanwhile, the rituals accumulate, drawing the couple ever closer to marriage, but at the same time they may feel strangely suspended between the old life and the new, belonging to neither.

Once a couple is formally engaged (even if only privately) the superstitions begin to gather strength, mainly on the basis of not jeopardising the future marriage by anticipating it. It is unlucky for an engaged couple to be **photographed** together, or to stand as **godparents** for the same child at a christening. An engaged girl would be unwise to knit her fiancé a **sweater**, or to sign her **married name** before the wedding day (or let anyone call her by it). She should not read the **wedding service** beforehand (she should use a proxy at wedding rehearsals) or assemble her **trousseau** before the wedding eve (remembering not to mark it with her married name).

In some parts of the world a girl cannot reject a suitor once she has accepted a gift of clothes from him. In Guernsey a **flouncing party** is equally binding – it is the occasion for meeting the future in-laws and, thereafter, any change of mind by either side loses them half their property.

In the early days of the Christian Church, the betrothal was sworn before witnesses as a formal contract and was so binding that, if one of the pair died before the wedding ceremony, part of the estate passed to the survivor.

In **China**, such an unfortunate death was often glossed over – a girl's wedding went ahead regardless and she was immediately treated as a widow.

By an ancient **Buddhist** custom, those who die too young to have married on earth are given a 'soul marriage' with the blessing of their families.

Right: Prince Charles and the then Lady Diana Spencer posing together for the first time in the grounds of Buckingham Palace, after the announcement of their plans to marry.

RING IN THE NEW

A betrothal or engagement is effectively a promise or contract to marry someone. The word 'troth' has links with 'truth' in the sense of faithfulness, constancy and fidelity. In **Ancient Rome**, the betrothal was a solemn contract, not between the couple but between their fathers or guardians and, as with all Roman contracts, it involved the making of a pledge. In this case, the giving of a **ring** served as a legal conclusion to pre-marriage bargaining. Thus the troth-ring became a sign of the betrothal contract. Many of the Roman troth-rings were designed as two right hands clasping each other (an action which was an integral gesture at the wedding ceremony) and they were often worn on the upper joint of the finger.

The **Ancient Greeks** probably did not have betrothal rings, and indeed only signet rings were worn until later in the period when rings started to be worn for personal adornment. By then they were often designed as snake-coils and similar designs were fashionable for bracelets, anklets and thigh-bands.

In Western cultures today, when courtship has become too serious for flippant love-tokens the gift of an **engagement ring** indicates that marriage is intended. The return of the ring is an emotional, if not legal, way of breaking the 'contract' of betrothal.

Most couples now choose a solitary **diamond** for the ring, as a symbol of faithfulness. In fact, it became a popular choice in the 19th century for a less romantic reason – South African imports were relatively cheap. Birthstones connected with each month are supposed to give the wearer special qualities, but only if the gem is the wearer's particular birthstone. The gems, and the qualities they are said to offer, are as follows:

JANUARY: Garnet (truth and faithfulness)
FEBRUARY: Amethyst (sincerity)
MARCH: Aquamarine (courage) or
              Bloodstone (strength)
APRIL: Diamond (love, innocence,
              light)
MAY: Emerald (happiness, hope, love,
              success)
JUNE: Agate (prosperity), Moonstone
              (love)
JULY: Ruby (fidelity, contentment,
              preservation of chastity) or
              Cornelian (calmness)
AUGUST: Sardonyx (marital bliss) or
              Peridot (inspiration)
SEPTEMBER: Sapphire (repentance and true
              love)
OCTOBER: Opal (love and loveliness)
NOVEMBER: Topaz (faithfulness)
DECEMBER: Turquoise (contentment,
              harmony, prosperity)

The **turquoise** is said to prevent marital arguments, while in America the **opal** represents instability and fickleness, and silvery **pearls** are tears. In Germany, brides hide pearls in a casket to avert tears.

According to Basque legend, Tartaro (the hideous equivalent of Cyclops) gave an irremovable talking ring to the girl he wanted to marry. As soon as she put it on, it began to repeat incessantly: 'You there, and I here.' Eventually, she could stand it no longer and cut off her own finger, throwing it, with the ring intact, into a pond.

In Swaziland, girls were not allowed to grow their hair long until they had definite prospects of becoming brides, after which they would proudly mould their hair into huge edifices stiffened with clay and grass, using porcupine quills to tease the hair into place.

At a formal Sikh betrothal ceremony, the girl's relations go to the boy's house and hand him a kirpan (a sword symbolic of dignity and respect) and one rupee in the presence of the Guru Granth Sahib (the main Sikh scripture); the boy's parents take the girl a dress and a gold ornament and (more recently) a ring.

The Victorians copied a Parisian fashion for rings in which the initials of a mixture of stones spelt a message:

DEAREST: Diamond, Emerald, Amethyst, Ruby, Emerald, Sapphire, Tourmaline
LOVE ME: Lapis lazuli, Opal, Verdantique, Emerald, Moonstone, Epidote
REGARD: Ruby, Emerald, Garnet, Amethyst, Ruby, Diamond

In Korea, men as well as women used to wear their hair long and dressed identically, in white, until they married.

TERMS OF ENDEARMENT

Marriage is essentially, but not solely, a contract. In **English** law, marriage is supposed to be voluntary, monogamous, and for life. The two parties enter into an agreement to marry and that agreement is registered and witnessed, be it in a church or at a civil ceremony. As soon as the marriage formally exists, each partner has legal status, and with that status come privileges which cohabiting partners, who are not married, do not enjoy. Because marriage is a legal contract, its dissolution cannot be by mutual consent alone. The alteration of the legal relationship has to be a matter for the courts.

By contrast, in **Islamic** law the husband merely states three times, before witnesses, 'I divorce you.' However, because part of the Islamic mar-

riage contract states that a husband is financially responsible for his wife's maintenance, he must provide her with suitable accommodation according to her wishes, and she is under no obligation to spend her own money or to earn a living.

Pre-nuptial divorce contracts, or at least premarital agreements, are becoming increasingly common in Britain. Before the wedding, financial agreements are put in writing so that, should the marriage break down, arguments and acrimony can be avoided – in theory, at least!

Such pre-nuptial agreements need not concern only finances. Some set out everything from sex to child-rearing and housework as couples concoct their recipe for a successful future together. Perhaps the greatest benefit is that, in devising the contract, the couple discuss their *real* expectations of the marriage and do not marry under false illusions. In this sense, it bears similarities to an arranged marriage. Some couples include a specified revision period, realising that their priorities may change during the marriage. Sometimes, the act of sorting out all the contract clauses helps the couple to realise that marriage is not a good idea after all!

Jewish couples are sometimes brought together through a professional matchmaker (*shadkhan*) but marriages are voluntary rather than arranged and are viewed as contractual relationships. A marriage document (*Ketuba*) is prepared before the wedding ceremony and, in essence, it provides the bride with an acceptable level of material security in the event of widowhood or the dissolution of the marriage. It is usually written in Aramaic.

As part of his marriage contract, a man of the West African **Wolof** tribe undertakes to work in his father-in-law's fields at certain times of year, build a new house for him or repair his roofs and

English law no longer sees breach of promise to marry as a suitable excuse for suing. In 1913, however, the 6th Marquess of Northampton (1885–1978) paid £50 000 for breach of promise to Miss Daisy Markham, later known as Mrs Annie Moss, who died in 1962 aged 76.

In the Sicilian town of Favera in 1990, a 24-year-old schoolteacher, Francesca Sanfilippo, changed her mind four days before her wedding and declared to her fiancé that she would enter a convent and become a nun because, she claimed, she was being forced into the marriage by her parents. An almighty row followed between the various relatives, and in the subsequent gunfight two men were killed and three more wounded. A shotgun wedding?

fences. Hard work is always highly esteemed – a champion worker easily wins the girl of his choice as long as both are of the same social level.

James Gordon Bennett Jnr (1841–1918) was the young multi-millionaire who financed Stanley to find Livingstone and supported Livingstone's Congo journeys (he also promoted Polar exploration). He was engaged to a girl whose family lived in New York's Fifth Avenue. On New Year's Day in 1877, he arrived at her parents' house, somewhat drunk, and found his way to the dining-room where, in front of everybody, he relieved himself in front of the fireplace. The engagement was promptly broken off and he spent the rest of his life as a fancy-free bachelor in Paris, thus depriving the US Treasury of millions of dollars in tax.

In June 1969, **Octavio Guillen** and **Adriana Martinez**, both at the age of 82, married in Mexico City, after an engagement which had lasted for 67 years. Needless to say, this is the current world record for the longest engagement.

Insurance brokers will now help you, or perhaps the bride's father, if he is footing most of the bills, to obtain cover against the postponement or abandonment of a wedding for reasons beyond everyone's control. Accident, illness or death of principal participants are covered, but if the cause is the deliberate failure of one partner to turn up on the day there can be no claim.

CHILD BRIDES

Under **English** law until 1929, any marriage of a boy younger than 14, or a girl younger than 12, was voidable. Since 1929, the law has stated that both parties must be at least 16 years old. 'Lunatics' cannot legally marry, but those not certified insane can marry 'during a lucid interval', or if the nature of the contract is clearly understood. It is essential under English law that the marriage should be entered into freely, without threat or compulsion.

The **lowest average age** of marriage in 1990 was found in India (20 for men, 14 for girls) and the highest was in Ireland (26.8 for men, 24.7 for women). Not much changes – in 1967, the same two countries featured in the records, but the average ages in Ireland at that time were even higher – 31.4 for men and 26.5 for women.

In the People's Republic of **China**, the officially recommended age for marriage was 28 for men and 25 for women. Even now, an unmarried woman over 28 is considered too old for marriage!

The **Rif** people of Morocco marry young – the girls at 15 and the boys between 15 and 18 – with the express intention of immediate and incessant child-bearing.

During the **Vedic** period in India, girls and boys used to take a vow of chastity for the duration of their compulsory spiritual education before the second stage of their life, which was marriage. In those days, girls were free to choose their own partners. However, during the **Smurti** period child marriage was practised and marriages were arranged while the children were babies, with top priority being given to compatibility between the in-laws. The young couple grew up together and were married before puberty. Child marriage is

The Maid of Norway was Margaret, daughter of King Eric II of Norway. Born in 1283, she was acknowledged as Queen of Scotland at the age of two, when her maternal grandfather, King Alexander III of Scotland, died. She was betrothed to Edward, son of England's King Edward I, but the little bride died on her voyage to Scotland when she was still only seven years old.

In 1986, it was reported that a family feud over a disputed farm in Bangladesh was patched up by marrying a three-month-old girl to an 11-month-old boy. This is the youngest marriage world record.

now illegal – a girl cannot marry until she is 14 years old.

Among the **Newars** of Nepal, a baby girl is 'married' to a bel fruit which is then cast into a sacred river. No one knows the fate of the fruit, so the girl can never become a widow.

On the **San Blas Islands** off the north coast of Panama, baby girls used to have their noses pierced for rings. They usually married at about 12 years old, when their hair was cut short and was never allowed to grow long again.

TESTING THE WATER

Christians tend to see three main reasons for marriage: the procreation of children, a proper relationship for sexual intercourse, and a framework for a couple's mutual society. Catholics emphasise the first reason, Anglicans the third.

However, marriage as a sacrament does not have an ancient history in the West. It was not until the 16th-century **Council of Trent** and the 18th-century **Marriage Act** that the Church and the State insisted on public ceremony and refused to recognise 'common law' marriages. Before then, as long as a man and a woman were betrothed, sexual intercourse was not regarded as sinful, and as long as two people were committed to each other by mutual consent they were regarded as married *because* they lived together. There is nothing new about 'living in sin'. Couples were expected to remain together for life – albeit that this might not have been very long because many women died in childbirth.

The **1753 Marriage Act** was made for bureaucratic rather than moral reasons, but it did specify that the exchange of consent between the couple had to be in a church before a priest and two witnesses. This condition was laid down despite protests that it was an unwarranted interference by church authorities in what was seen as the freedom of a Christian to marry. Marriage, many argued (and many still do), is a matter of private consent between two individuals, and in fact that is what Christian theology traditionally taught. The legal status of marriage had nothing to do with Christian doctrine.

However, **strict monogamy** has been the essence of the marital contract, private or public, since the time of pre-Christian Judaism and remains so in Christianity today, though there is no *direct* New Testament teaching on the subject. Today there seems to be an increasing trend for 'consecutive monogamy' or 'serial polygamy' as the divorce rates rise and people marry again.

During the 'Swinging 60s' in Britain, only a very small minority of couples cohabited as a prelude to legal marriage, but the idea became more popular in the 1970s and by the 1980s it had virtually become the accepted practice. In 1987, 48% of married women said they had lived with their partners before marriage, compared with only 19% in the late 1970s. By 1987, 17% of single women were cohabiting – more than twice as many as in 1981 – and now more than a quarter of all children in this country are born out of wedlock, with 68% of such births being registered by both parents, of whom half live at the same address.

'Living in sin' is therefore no longer a furtive way of life. It is now more likely to involve the highly educated and successful rather than the poor who have no family support. Various groups are working on **cohabitation contracts** to protect the children of such arrangements as well as the partners. Councils for one-parent families already

The English Law Commission feels that the chances of people getting a share in property to which they have contributed are already very good under English law, but some would not agree. For example, Victoria Windeler shared a home with theatrical agent Michael Whitehall for ten years, helping him to build up his business by giving him domestic support, but in 1989 a High Court judge told her it was 'ridiculous' to expect a share of the home when they split up.

encourage couples to draw up pre-cohabitation contracts but warn against the problems of doing so when judgement is clouded by being 'in love'. The **Family Law Reform Act** does now allow certain property transfers and claims, while the **Family Policy Studies Unit** (partly funded by the Government) is undertaking a major study on cohabitation, which its director, Malcolm Wicks, sees as 'the most significant social change of the generation'.

The **Scottish Law Commission** is seeking views on whether cohabiting couples should be covered by family law, particularly in cases where a partner has helped in building up a business, home or family, and is left with no legal right to compensation or maintenance if the relationship fails.

Under English law, unmarried **cohabitees** are not well protected when the relationship breaks down. The law says that men have no legal obligation to support their mistresses, even if they are living with them. However, in certain American states, cohabitation contracts and 'palimony' payments *are* recognised.

Mistresses who are not actually living with their long-term lovers have even fewer rights when the relationship ends. Unlike cohabitants, they are not

Handfasting was a very sensible Anglo-Saxon custom. The couple joined hands and vowed to be faithful to each other for a year and a day. When this trial period was over, they could either dissolve their 'marriage' or confirm it with formal nuptials. There was a similar tradition in Ancient Rome – if the couple had lived together without being separated for more than three nights in their year together, they were considered to be married.

Handfasting continued as a tradition until medieval times, when the Church incorporated it into ecclesiastical law, though the older non-Church custom continued and was legal and binding, though 'improper'. In Dumfriesshire there used to be Handfasting Fairs at which young men chose women they would like to live with in a handfast wedding.

Landscapes sometimes feature stones with natural holes – a phenomenon which was believed to give them magical properties. The ancient tradition of marrying 'through the stone' involved couples clasping hands through the hole and making their vows. In the Orkneys, such pledges were made through the Woden Stone or the Standing Stones of Stennis, but could be revoked if the couple attended a service at a Christian church and then left the building by separate doors.

covered by the **1976 Domestic Violence** legislation, nor are contracts drawn up with their lovers deemed to be legally enforceable. Their only recompense is the **1975 Inheritance Act** in which the lover's estate can provide for a mistress's continued maintenance. A mistress, however faithful she might be (and many are as loyal as any wife), is still described by one law lord as a woman 'installed in a clandestine way by someone of substance, normally married, for his intermittent sexual enjoyment' – which greatly belittles the mistress and is a very outdated definition.

In **Bolivia**, there is a long tradition of trial marriages for young couples to allow them to prove that they are compatible and both capable of hard work on the land. They might or might not become formally married in due course, and it is not considered improper for the couple to have children outside of wedlock. It is quite acceptable to have two attempts at such trial marriages, but a third smacks of promiscuity.

In **France**, a gypsy woman might reveal her desire to live with a man by breaking a clay pot before him. She undertakes to stay with him for as many years as there are broken pieces, and thereafter they can either separate or break another pot to extend the contract.

In **Japan**, there are three-day 'rent marriages'. The woman is ceremonially escorted to her partner's house and stays with him for three days. Both partners are on approval – if they like each other, they can continue to live together or become formally united. If not, there is no disgrace and they tactfully agree to separate.

Bundling, also known as queesting or bed-fellowship, was the art of combining practicality (keeping warm) with the thrill of cuddling (but without intercourse). An unmarried couple shared a bed but there was a barrier between them – either a board or a bolster (or, in traditional 'proxy' marriages, a sword). Alternatively, the couple were both fully dressed and the girl was 'bundled' in clothing which, in theory, made her inaccessible. Typically, her mother would dress her in a bundling stocking – a tight, full-length tube of skirt – or lots of extra petticoats, sometimes knotted. The poor girl may even have had her legs tied together! The custom was widespread for many centuries in Europe and also in New England, in America – even the early Puritans permitted bundling, partly to keep warm and partly to save a few trees by having fewer beds!

Among the Kikuyu tribe of Kenya, bundling is a sophisticated game known as *ngweko*, which starts as a group meeting at which boys and girls choose partners and eventually lie together, the boy naked but the girl wearing a protectively tied leather apron.

3
And So To Wed...

TIMING IT RIGHT

Throughout central Europe in particular, the advice has always been: **'Don't marry in May.'** May is the time, it is said, when whores and knaves go to church and every ass is in love; May is the season of cuckoos and cuckolds. The superstition against May marriages dates at least as far back as Roman times, when it was the month for extra-marital sex.

In Britain, the **close seasons** for marriage used to be from **Advent** to **St Hilary's Day** (13th

Marry in September's shine, your living will be rich and fine;

If in October you do marry, love will come but riches tarry;

If you wed in bleak November, only joy will you remember;

When December's showers fall fast, marry and true love will last.

January), from **Septuagesima** to **Low Sunday**, and from **Rogation Sunday** to **Trinity Sunday**. These rules were strictly applied at the time of the Reformation.

> 'Advent marriage doth thee deny,
> But Hilary gives thee liberty.
> Septuagesima says thee nay,
> Eight days from Easter says you may.
> Rogation bids thee to contain,
> But Trinity sets thee free again.'

Advent and **Easter Week** used to be avoided as unlucky times for weddings, but **Easter** itself is now popular.

The Roman Catholic Church does not allow nuptial mass between the **first Sunday in Advent** and the **Octave of the Epiphany**, or from **Ash Wednesday** to **Low Sunday**.

In **Judaism**, certain times of year are carefully avoided, such as the first nine days of the Hebrew month of **Av**, and most of the period between **Passover** and **Pentecost**. Weddings cannot take place on the **Sabbath** or during major festivals.

Hindus take the advice of the family priest who looks for a time when the stars are in an exalted position – certain months of the year are generally avoided. In India, marriages take place mainly during **Uttarayan** (when the sun is in the northern hemisphere) and in the **Shuklapksha** (when the moon is waxing during the first fortnight of the month).

In Ancient China, the marriage season was from shortly after the **autumn equinox** until just after the **spring equinox**, and any young people still unwed towards the end of that period were urgently encouraged to marry. The ideal Chinese wedding date was at the **first new moon** of the new Chinese year, or when the first **peach blossoms** emerged.

These days, the **Chinese** are careful to consult astrological charts and the precise hour is chosen. If the moment is missed, the couple must wait for another auspicious time even if it means a delay of years.

> *Marry when the year is new,*
> *Always loving, always true.*

> *Marriages made in May last for only one summer.*

> *Marry in May, rue for aye.*

Scorpio, the eighth sign of the zodiac, which the sun enters about 23rd/24th October, is said by some to rule the loins and thus bring an auspicious time for marriage.

In the **Swiss Alps**, weddings did not take place during the sickle-cut hay harvest (everybody was too busy) and likewise, in Ireland and many other countries, scythe-cut grain harvest times were avoided.

> *They that wive*
> *between sickle and scythe*
> *shall never thrive.*

The **solar eclipse** is thought to be a bad omen for a wedding day. A **waxing moon** in late autumn was considered auspicious in Ancient Rome, as was a **full moon** in winter in Ancient Greece. In Germany, a **harvest moon** in September is thought ideal for a wedding. In several cultures, a **waning moon** at the time of the marriage is seen as a blight on its future happiness or fruitfulness. An **ebbing tide**, likewise, renders a marriage unfruitful – to be sure of riches and children make sure it is rising during the wedding ceremony.

DAY DREAMS

Friday was considered the luckiest day of the week for a Norseman's wedding (it was sacred to Freyja and therefore lucky for lovers) but it was deemed unlucky among Buddhists and Brahmins. To marry on **Friday 13th** is thought very unlucky in Britain because it is widely believed to have been the date of Christ's crucifixion.

"

Monday for wealth; Tuesday for health;
Wednesday the best day of all;
Thursday for losses; Friday for crosses;
and Saturday no luck at all!

"

Local customs vary: some say that **Wednesday** weddings invite poverty, but in most places **Monday** and **Tuesday** are considered lucky days for weddings. **Thursday** was considered a good day in Northamptonshire and Shropshire.

In Britain, certain days in the calendar are traditionally avoided for weddings. These include: **St Swithun's Day** (15th July), **Maundy Thursday** (in Holy Week) and **Childermas** (28th December, also known as Holy Innocents' Day, when Herod slaughtered the children) or indeed even the weekday on which the previous Childermas fell. Sometimes **St Thomas's Day** (21st December) was avoided, especially in Yorkshire where it was believed to lead to early widowhood. However, in Lancashire it was thought to be a good day because, as the shortest day of the year, it left 'less time for repentance'!

In Italy, **Sunday** is best, **Monday** promises you idiot children or daughters, **Tuesday** a clubfooted first son, **Wednesday** and **Friday** are fast days, and **Thursday** is for witches.

Ian and Sonia Phillips married at Christchurch, Cheltenham, on 21st April, 1990, and the very next day they both ran in the tenth London Marathon instead of going on honeymoon. They had set the date a year before, not knowing when the marathon would be. 'We both do a lot of sport,' said Ian, an industrial engineer, 'so our friends weren't too surprised. It just meant going easy on the champagne.'

In Cuba, 14th February is known as Loving Day and it is an overwhelmingly popular date for weddings at the huge Palacios de los Matrimonios, which sometimes handles more than a hundred on that day – three or four times as many as usual.

On 18th August, 1572, Henry of Navarre married Margaret of Valois. It came to be known as the Blood-Red Wedding – it was followed a week later by the Massacre of St Bartholomew.

Simon Weston had 46% of his body horrifically burned during the Falklands campaign. For his wedding he deliberately chose the date exactly eight years to the day after that nightmarish event in 1982 – he wanted his new life as a married man to be as happy as it had been before the Falklands.

THE BUILD-UP

In Britain, a girl planning a white wedding must make endless preparations. If she is well organised she starts about six months before the wedding day by contacting the church's minister, booking the honeymoon, preparing the guest list, booking the reception venue and caterers, choosing her attendants and considering their outfits. With five months to go, she is thinking about booking an interesting vehicle to take her to and from the church, and choosing professional photographers. She also begins to make up a gift list so that, with luck, she will get one of everything she wants rather than six useless items. At the four-month stage it is time for the couple to talk to the minister about banns, service sheets, bell-ringing, church flowers, choir and so on. It is also time to order wedding stationery, discuss bouquets with the florist and buy wedding rings. At three months they are sorting out where to stay on the wedding night, completing the honeymoon plans, making sure passports are valid and thinking about their 'going away' outfits. With two months left they are sending out the invitations and beginning to receive presents as well as choosing gifts for the bridesmaids, ushers and best man.

Good grief, what a performance! No wonder weddings can be so expensive and times of such tension. The superstitious would be appalled – there is a strong traditional instinct against counting chickens before they hatch, and the malignant imps grow more and more alert to opportunities for mischief as 'The Big Day' approaches.

ALL IN PLACE

Seven out of ten first marriages in Britain today involve a **church** ceremony. Weddings have been held in **registry offices** since the time of King William IV and although they were rare before the 20th century, they have increased rapidly since the end of the Second World War. Under English law before 1990, marriages had to be solemnised by either a duly ordained clergyman of the Established Church, or some other person authorised under the Marriage Act of 1898 to solemnise a marriage in a building certified by law as a place of worship; or by a registrar in a registry office.

Since 1990, it has been legal for a couple to marry anywhere they choose. The English can be

The old rhyme, 'Change the name not the letter, change for the worse not the better,' is based on ancient prejudices against intermarriage between related clans. But oddly, in parts of England, women whose surname remained the same on marriage (as long as they had not married a relative) were supposed to have healing powers.

The average cost of a British wedding in 1990 was about £6500. That is an increase of £1200 on the cost in 1989 and it is set to rise further. Even a small wedding might cost about £4000. No wonder the insurance companies are making a killing!

Electrical contractor Roy Watson and secretary Julie Anne Matcham, both from the Hampshire town of Petersfield, held their wedding on the beach of the Indian Ocean island of Mauritius in the summer of 1990, but to do so they had to obtain temporary citizenship of the island. The local hotel presented them with the use of the VIP suite for their honeymoon.

In August 1990, thousands of US Marines suddenly found themselves departing for Saudi Arabia to stand by for a possible war in the Gulf. In the Marines' chapel at Twentynine Palms, California, five times more weddings than average were performed in the week of their departure, including that of Airman First Class Wade West, recalled from leave on 7th August, who married and left for the Gulf within the hour. President Bush remarked: 'You're talking about a guy that gets things done.'

This sign in Las Vegas is designed to catch the eye of the matrimonially minded interested in a quick, cheap wedding – the sign is even illuminated at night.

In February 1985, Randall Chambers and Patricia Manuel were married at the South Pole at a temperature of −45°C (−49°F). They had met while working for the American Antarctic 'Operation Deep Freeze' (not, one hopes, a bad omen).

as imaginative as the Americans and, as well as hotels and country houses, some couples are choosing to marry on top of mountains, under the sea and even in mid-air, in fact anywhere the registrar or parson can be persuaded to attend.

In **Scotland**, a clergyman was not restricted to churches as wedding venues, even before 1990, and private houses have long been popular backgrounds for wedding ceremonies. Glasgow's **Bur-**

lington House, in Bath Street, had a suite of rooms so that the ceremony and the celebrations could be held under the same roof.

After due notice to the Superintendent Registrar, members of the **Society of Friends** (ie Quakers) can marry in a Friends' meeting-house.

Jews in Britain can be married in a synagogue or private house by the secretary of the synagogue to which the husband belongs.

A nice idea from a wedding in Toronto – the whole affair was held on a moving streetcar, which collected the participants and guests from various stops along the route. (No, the streetcar was *not* named Desire.)

In January 1846, it was snowing heavily in Wisconsin on the day that Joseph Hill was due to wed Lydia M Warren of Hubbard. The officiator, Barnabus Snow(!), was snowbound 13 miles (20 km) away. Fortunately, Joseph was a Justice of the Peace and realised that he could actually officiate at his own wedding ceremony.

Salim Abu Samra and Rita Zgheib married in Zalka, north of Beirut, in April 1990. The ceremony had to wait for a brief lull in the fighting between rival Christian militia, and the couple wore flak-jackets over their wedding clothes.

Li Lu, one of the leaders of the Chinese students in the Peking demonstrations, married his Nanjing girlfriend Zhao Ming on impulse on 21st May, 1989, in Tiananmen Square. The joyous crowd sang the Wedding March, toasted the couple with salt water and managed to find all sorts of small gifts – even leaflets if they had no sweets, pens or clothes to give. 'I'm 23 years old,' said Li Lu. 'In my short life, I've experienced everything but sex and marriage. I may die at any time. I owe myself this pleasure!' Fellow leader Chai Ling had already told the crowd, 'We have to fight, but we must marry too,' and the crowd took up her words as a chant at the wedding ceremony. The infamous massacre came a few days later, on 4th June, just after Chai Ling had celebrated her own first wedding anniversary.

LICENSED TO THRILL

The calling of **banns** was instituted in the 12th century. In England, the Marriage Act of 1753 insisted on the public calling of banns unless a special licence had been granted. The banns are called in the parish church for three successive Sundays, usually after the second lesson in the morning service. The parish must be the one in which the parties have resided for at least 15 days prior to the marriage, and the wedding must take place within three months of the banns being published.

Residential qualifications also apply to **registry office** weddings. To qualify for a **Superintendent Registrar's licence**, one party must have resided in the district for at least 15 days. Alternatively, seven days' residence grants a cheaper certificate although this does not become effective until 21 days after the notice is given.

There are, of course, superstitions surrounding banns. It was thought unlucky to have them called partly in one year and partly in the next, and it was believed that the first child of a bride who heard her own banns would be an idiot or deaf mute. Not only was it considered bad luck to cancel the wedding after the third reading of the banns, in the 19th century the couple were fined for such an affront to the community! In some places, a peal of church bells followed the third reading, to drive out any evil influences and bless the couple.

However, there are alternatives to banns. Marriage can be by **special licence** granted by the Archbishop of Canterbury, in which case the wedding can take place at any time or place without residential qualification. An **ordinary licence** entitles a couple to marry in church without previous notice, as long as one party has resided within the parish for the 15 days preceding the issue of the licence. That party must declare on oath that there is no legal impediment to the marriage.

Any couple aged over 16 can marry at a registry office. The registrar will have an initial interview with them, taking down details of full names, addresses, ages, occupations, and whether either has been married before. He ensures that their marriage is a voluntary union for both partners. A date is then agreed for the wedding ceremony, at which the couple marry each other in the presence of witnesses while the registrar is the celebrant and registers their act of marriage.

THE WEDDING EVE

The eve of the wedding marks the imminence of stepping out of the old life forever and into the new and unknown. It is a time for excitement, anticipation and – for some – sheer terror!

The most familiar tradition in the West is the **stag party** at which the groom and his friends are usually well lubricated with alcohol. If possible, the groom is made to look a fool in a final light-hearted attempt to bar his way to marriage. Superstition has it that noise is essential on the wedding eve as this is a particularly dangerous time of transit and evil spirits must be frightened off – and it provides a good excuse for the singing, glass-breaking and crockery-smashing which might ensue.

In the **Middle East**, noise is important for keeping the groom and the bride awake and on their guard against spirits during the night before the wedding.

In some places, the wedding eve is a time for ritual **washing** of the bride and groom, especially their feet, so that they can walk fresh-footed into their new life. Footwashing is known in Scotland (the bride's friends wash hers), Java (the bride washes the groom's) and Iran (mutual footwashing between bride and groom). A Jewish bride is given a ritual bath or *mikvah*.

A bride in **Ancient Greece** followed several rituals on the day before her wedding. She would offer her childhood playthings to the deities, especially to Artemis, goddess of the moon. She would also have a ritual bath in water brought to her in a special tall vase (*loutrophoros*) by a procession of women, who would then help her dress for the wedding. They would also turn a magic wheel to inspire the bridegroom with greater longing to love her. Accompanied by his best man (*parochos*), he would come to fetch her at nightfall and take her by torchlight in a mule-drawn cart to his parents' home for the ceremony.

For a **Hindu** wedding, the families and friends get together and make what is necessary for the ceremony, such as special sweets and decorations of pearls, beads and scented flowers to crown the bride and her groom.

WEDDING PRESENTS

Love-in-a-cottage is a term to denote marriage for love, without sufficient means to maintain social status – very romantic but far from practical. If there are no dowries to help the couple on their way, they need the gifts of their friends and relatives as the basis of their new household.

In many countries around the world, the custom involves the collection of **money** from all who attend the wedding festivities and sometimes this is made into entertainment by pinning banknotes to the bride's dress as she dances, perhaps, or by having fund-raising games and sports. **Penny weddings** were held in Scotland and Wales for impoverished couples – each guest contributed up to a shilling towards the expense of the wedding celebrations, and any money left over helped the newlyweds to furnish their new home.

In **Britain**, the wedding gifts are usually laid out on display for all to see. In several countries there are traditional ways of transferring the gifts to the bride's home as a rite of passage. In **Finland**, the bride gathers them into a pillowcase and makes a slow procession to her new abode, accompanied by a protective elderly man wearing a top hat and carrying an umbrella. In **Scotland**, the bride's gifts and trousseau are packed into a special chest or kist, which the bride locks, giving the key to the best man to keep for the duration of the journey from her parents' house to her new home. In **Italy**, the bride's friends inspect the gifts closely and then carry them to her new home. In northern **France**, the gifts are put in a carved chest and transported in a painted wagon.

In some African tribes, brides used to be deliberately fattened before the marriage.

Traditionally, beekeepers prepare white ribbons on the eve of a household wedding and then tie them to the hive on the wedding day while they 'tell the bees' of this important family event. It is said that failure to keep bees informed drives them away!

Gifts being delivered to a Chinese bride's house (c. 1845). The bride is preparing for her wedding (right) in the presence of weeping women.

Bridal showers are popular in the **USA**, where groups of friends give the bride small gifts – perhaps on a particular theme such as clothes or kitchenware. Lucky brides are given several showers.

In **Ancient Greece**, wedding presents were received on the day *after* the wedding, when friends and relations brought them to the husband's house. They were usually practical items for the bride, such as spinning equipment, toilet articles and vases.

More superstitions! In general, pointed or sharp gifts are considered unlucky in case they 'cut' the

It is sometimes said that the 'seven-year itch', which so often disrupts a marriage, arises at this point because it is when the wedding gifts are reaching the end of their useful life and need replacing . . .

romance, and should only be given in exchange for a penny. However, symbolic gifts were common and a pair of scissors, for example, was given to 'cut the threads of love' should the husband prove untrue to his bride.

In 1910, a Hertfordshire bride, the daughter of a blacksmith, was given a pig as a wedding present, and a very good investment it was, too! It had produced 28 piglets by the time of the couple's first wedding anniversary. Several decades later another woman, Susan Hulme, was given an Ayrshire cow as a wedding present. As a result of the excess milk it produced she developed a smallholding with pigs to lap it up, and eventually wrote a delightful and informative book about keeping and breeding pigs.

CATCHING THE BRIDE

Ever since the proverbial caveman grabbed his woman by her hair and dragged her into his cave, brides have been captured as well as bought. Some say that the folk-memory of **bride-capture** is largely responsible for the music-hall hostility between husbands and their mothers-in-law. The traditional surrounding of bride and groom with their own parties of attendants certainly has something to do with the ancient hostility between the 'opposing' sides. No doubt this led to the system of bartering for a bride, with the bride's kin requiring payment for letting the girl join the man's group.

There are examples of bride-capture to be found all over the world, though today the 'capture' is more often a ritual or a hearty game than a serious abduction. In Greek mythology the **Centaur** (half man, half horse) would often abduct brides or betrothed girls, and it is this which lies behind a long tradition of mock bride-capture by men on horseback, in countries as far removed as Africa and Celtic Wales.

In Celtic folklore, fairies used to abduct brides, but in Wales in the 18th century they had **horse weddings** where the groom and his friends would mount their horses on the wedding morning and demand the bride. Her party would refuse to hand her over and, during the mock battle that ensued, the bride would mount a horse behind her nearest male relative and be carried away, with the groom's party in hot pursuit, whooping and shouting loudly as they galloped. Sometimes these cheerfully noisy chases involved literally hundreds of local people. In due course, naturally, the bride would be captured or 'saved' by her groom, and led home in triumph to a wedding feast.

A similar custom in Ireland was known as '**dragging home the bride**' and it involved dart-throwing, reminiscent of a mythological spear-throwing contest in the Celtic story of Kulhwch and Olwen. The custom lapsed, however, after Lord Howth lost an eye to a dart during these shenanigans in the late 17th century. In Africa, some tribes still loose off their spears at wedding ceremonies in an attempt to frighten off bad spirits.

Traditional Turkoman bride chase, c. 1860. The custom of the bridegroom's party pursuing a 'reluctant' bride on horseback was still common in many countries in the 19th century.

In Iceland, the very word for marriage – *brudlaup* – means 'bride-run'. In Poland, the ancient custom of bearing away the bride persists even now, and she is expected to weep copiously even if her tears are false.

In Wales, it is traditional for the groom to answer a series of **riddles**, or take part in a contest of verse for several hours on the doorstep of the bride's home. Riddle contests are also traditional to the marriage rituals in parts of Russia and central Asia.

Even when the riddles have been solved, grooms in Wales and in many other European countries have further hurdles. For example, the bride might be disguised when the groom comes to collect her – perhaps as an old woman, or hidden behind a curtain with friends – and he is offered a **false bride**. In Brittany, the groom would first be shown a young girl, then the mistress of the house, then the grandmother, and in other places he is offered a doll or even a bearded man! Eventually he finds his bride and carries her off to the church on horseback. Her family and friends pursue them but he ensures that they do not actually come close enough to 'rescue' her.

Sometimes a young West African man of the **Wolof** tribe, frustrated by a girl's parents' refusal to let her go to his compound even though all the brideprice has been paid, will arrange for his work group to capture the girl as she visits the village well. However, this is usually done with her compliance. The men carry her off either on horseback or on their shoulders, while girls from her own group chase after them, shouting in good-natured protest. Usually the reason for the parents' reluctance is that they have been unable to get together the household articles and clothing a bride should take with her to her new home.

In **Connecticut**, USA, in the 18th century, the groom had a different hurdle to contend with – he would jokingly be dragged away from the altar itself by his own men in a final attempt to thwart the marriage. In other states the bride's rejected suitors would kidnap her and keep her hidden until the groom paid for her release by providing them with a good meal.

The native customs in **Bolivia** encourage a harmonious union between a man and woman, but it is believed that the conquering Spaniards upset the situation by introducing the concept of 'machismo' (exaggerated male pride) and subsequently, bride-capture. This involved the man going to the house of a girl (often as young as 14) and making an offer to marry her. A few days later he would return and carry her off to a family party where she would be given lots of alcohol by his relatives before he took her to bed.

MAIDS AND MEN

Traditionally, the important role of the bridesmaids, best man and ushers has been to protect the couple from **evil spirits** intent on doing mischief, as they always are at times of major change in a person's life, be it hatch, match or dispatch.

Until 50 years ago, a **Zulu** bride would carry a spear, dancing shield and stick to fight off the spirits, and wear a veil to protect herself from them. She also wore the bladders of goats or sheep which had been sacrificed to her ancestral spirits and she took care to have a ritual bath before her marriage. The prettier the bride, the more bridesmaids she needed to guard her, though they might not have been very fit to do so as they would have indulged in a two-day beer festival before the wedding day, to help inspire the verses they composed for the bridegroom. However, they swept the air with their brooms and brandished their spears and war-clubs to drive off the spirits, while groups of warriors, ahead of the bridal procession, also cleared the air of adverse spirits. The witchdoctor did everything in his power, both before and after

The best man played a major role in the days of real or mock bride-capture, when he no doubt earned his traditional gift from the groom rather more worthily than he does now. (The groom's gifts to the bridesmaids could be seen as either a bribe or a thank-you for 'releasing' the bride to him.)

Bachelor fishmonger Willy Gant certainly earned his rewards – he was best man 50 times from 1931 to 1964 – but his record was completely shattered by Ting Ming Siong of Sibu, in Malaysia, who, in March 1990, was best man for the 561st time since 1976.

the wedding ceremony, to repel the evil spirits.

In the West, the superstitious believe that the bride's procession to the church is fraught with difficulties. Traditionally, she surrounds herself with a protective group of friends and relatives. It used to be the custom for the bride to walk to church with the **best man**, followed by the groom, and accompanied by a **bridesmaid**, along a path strewn with protective rushes and herbs. On leaving the church, the bride and groom preceded the best man and bridesmaid, but it was said that 'those who walk to church together beforehand will never become man and wife' – that is to say, the best man would never marry the bridesmaid. Some people also say, 'Three times a bridesmaid, never a bride,' because a bridesmaid supposedly cushions the bride from the bad luck wished upon her by evil spirits, so that the more often a girl is a bridesmaid, the more bad luck she absorbs.

GET ME TO THE CHURCH
On the wedding day itself, superstitions abound – even getting to the church can be a risky business. **Walking** to church is considered better than riding because it gives more opportunity for omens to be observed on the way, and to protect the couple during such a dangerous 'journey', it is traditional for the bridesmaids to dress like the bride while the best man and ushers dress like the

The old Roman custom was for a group of bachelors to lead the bride to her wedding, but afterwards she was led home by a party of married men.

groom in order to confuse the spirits. (In old Danzig, Poland, men and women so dressed took part in a traditional wedding **dance**, each carrying a small tray bearing candles and a figurine of the bride or groom.) In Britain, before this century, it was said that no person, dog or cat should run between the two groups on the way to church, and in some places it is so important to avoid the separation of the couple at this stage that the bride and groom walk together, pressing close to each other and keeping their eyes downcast to avoid glancing at each other.

In China, a man with a **mirror** precedes the bride to deflect the 'evil eye' away from her, while in Sweden the bride wears glittering **ornaments** and shiny **bells** for the same reason. A Swedish groom and bridesmaids wear or carry particular **herbs** to protect the couple from bad fairies and witches. In Germany, the bride trusts to **dill** and **salt**, dropped into her shoes by her mother, while in the Near East, **salt** is thrown over the heads of the party. In many countries, symbols of good luck and fertility, such as **grain, flowers, nuts** and **cakes**, are carried or scattered ahead of the bridal procession.

In Bulgaria, it is traditional for the best man to lead a **goat** with gilded horns in front of the procession. It is said that this invites future wealth, and in many parts of Europe, **fiddlers** are popular leaders of wedding processions.

Bad omens en route include seeing a **pig** or **hare** or **lizard** running across the route, or catching sight of a **funeral** or an **open grave**. Needless to say, the sound of a funeral bell tolling for a dead wife is not a good sign.

By association, meeting a **nun** or **monk** on the way foretells barrenness and charity, while meeting a **cripple** suggests deformed children.

However, it need not be all doom and gloom. Seeing a **rainbow**, having the **sun** shine on the bride, meeting a **black cat** (or a white one,

In Syria, the groom makes sure that his bride does not pass a bakery on the way to the ceremony, which would induce future gluttony on her part!

This English bride and groom are met by a 'lucky' black cat on the steps of the church. From Picture Post, 20 February, 1954.

In many places it is considered unlucky to pass through the church's lychgate, which is the entrance for funeral processions, or the north door. At Hoxne in Suffolk, bridal processions carefully avoid the Gold Bridge, and in other parishes there are local superstitions about the route a procession should take. Sometimes it is necessary to take long detours to avoid unlucky landmarks.

During the ceremony itself, a German couple would consider it unlucky if the priest sneezes and in several countries it is unlucky if a clock chimes.

depending on which country you are in) and meeting a **chimney sweep** are all considered good omens. Meeting an elephant is thought fortunate, if a little unlikely!

In the West, many brides now ride to church rather than walk. Ideally the carriage should be drawn by **grey horses** wearing bright horse-brasses to deflect evil spirits, and a scarlet harness as protection against witches. It is a bad omen if the horses refuse to start the journey (the same is now said of the car). At the church, after the bride has alighted from the carriage, the driver must take his rig some distance before turning the animals' heads: it brings bad luck to the marriage if the carriage turns within sight of the couple. In Normandy, the horses must walk on the way to the church but must trot home afterwards.

> **"**
>
> *It won't be a stylish marriage,*
> *I can't afford a carriage,*
> *But you'll look sweet upon the seat*
> *Of a bicycle made for two.*
>
> Harry Dacre, *Daisy Bell*
>
> **"**

RAIN OR SHINE
Naturally, wedding-day weather provides plenty of scope for myth and superstition. All over the world brides hope for **sunshine** on their wedding day – the sun is generally associated with sexual stimulation and thus future fertility. In Scotland, it was traditional for the bride to 'walk with the sun', proceeding from east to west on the south side of the church and then circling the building three times 'sunwise' for luck. In South America, a marriage in the Chaco tribe is not formalised until the sun has shone on the newlywed couple's feet the following morning.

Rain on the wedding day is equated with either tears or fertility and some see it as lucky if rain falls on the bridal wreath. If a **thunderstorm** occurs during the wedding, a childless marriage is foretold, but **snow** is a blessing, equated with a shower of riches.

In North America, the wedding-day weather forecasts the future of the marriage from the bride's point of view – a fine morning suggests a good beginning but a stormy afternoon means rough times later in the marriage. The groom's future is forecast by the weather on the day *after* the wedding, while the weather on the third day foretells their joint future. If it is sunny, the prognostication for the marriage is calm, but a dark sky promises quarrels ahead.

BARRING THE WAY
The widespread custom of 'barring the way' is a final attempt to put difficulties in the path of the bride and groom and also to signify the rites of passage from one lifestyle to another. Marriage is a major step in anybody's life and the couple must 'pay' to join the new society of which they are becoming a part.

I just hope she's worth the effort!

Wedding 2pm

Typical obstacles are locked **gates**, interwoven **brambles**, **rope** barriers, **chains** and **sticks**. These either impede the groom on his way to the church or bar the couple as they try to leave after the ceremony. They then have to pay a **forfeit** for free passage and safe conduct, often to the accompaniment of plenty of noise (gunshots, bells, shouting) to deter those omnipresent evil spirits. The forfeit might be to contribute money for drinks so that the couple can be toasted. Sometimes the bride (and perhaps the groom and the guests as well) is expected to **jump** the obstacle, or be lifted over it by her new husband. The obstacle in question may be a special **petting stone** (petting, in this context, is not cuddling but refers to the bouts of sulks which she is expected to leave behind her on marriage), or a carpeted church stool. In Northumberland, it is customary for everybody to jump over a bench while complimentary verses are recited to the couple. This is known as 'saying the noning' and the groom usually pays the reciters in silver. The **gaudy loup** is a 'joyful leap' over a watercourse, usually a ford which the groom must wade through or jump across.

Among European gypsies there is a form of marriage ceremony referred to as 'jumping the broomstick' because, originally, the barrier was a green, flowering branch of broom. Holding hands, the couple must leap high over it – if the man's trousers brush the broom, it is said he will be an unfaithful husband; and if the woman's skirt does so, she is already pregnant, or has at least lost her virginity. After jumping, the bride is given the token of a finger-ring woven from rushes until the time the couple can afford a gold ring.

In Wales, the custom was to 'jump the besom', a birch-twig broom set across the open doorway of the bride's home, or the nuptial home. The bride and groom jumped over it into the house, making sure they touched neither the broom nor the doorpost. If this ceremony was performed in front of witnesses, the marriage was valid. However, it could later be dissolved if the dissatisfied partner jumped out of the house backwards over the besom, again in front of witnesses and without touching it. In Yorkshire, an unmarried mother is said to have jumped the besom, and a girl who unwittingly steps over the handle of a broom is destined to become a mother before being a wife.

COLOUR CODE

Marry in **blue**, they say, and you will always be true – every bride knows that she must at least have 'something blue' about her person. **Green**, however, has always been associated with the dangerous month of May, the month of out-of-doors extramarital lovemaking, which bodes no good at all for conjugality. In some places it was thought such an unlucky colour that not a touch of green was allowed at the wedding, not even in the decorations or the food.

Those dressed in blue have lovers true, But green and white, forsaken quite.

In China, the traditional lucky wedding colour is **red**. The bride wears a red jacket and trousers, with a veil like a lampshade to hide her face from the groom – even the marriage certificate is on red paper! White has always been associated with funerals but sophisticated modern Chinese brides now wear white dresses in Western styles – at least for their studio photographs.

Yellow is avoided by most of the world's brides, though the Roman girls wore yellow shoes and a yellow hairnet, and in 19th-century America the colour was said to attract lovers (a bride would wear a yellow garter to guarantee the wedding of a close friend within the year). Most brides also avoid the mourning colours of **purple** and **black**, though in Iceland early in this century the typical bride's outfit was of black velvet richly embroidered with gold and silver thread. In Victorian times, when royal weddings had set a precedent for white for society brides, those who were in a period of mourning wore **lavender** or **grey**.

A bride who marries in brown in Oxfordshire is told that she will 'never live in a town', which she might or might not see as a misfortune, though the rhyme is intended to imply that her husband will never have a successful career.

The colour **violet** is sometimes said to represent a 'love of truth and truth of love'.

Hindu brides never wear **white** or **black**, but the choice of other colours depends on local preference. There are between 300 and 400 different dialects in India, 14 major languages and 23 states, each with its own customs, and as individual as each nation in Europe.

NUPTIAL KNOTS

Knots are highly symbolic in many traditions. An **Islamic** groom, for example, carefully checks his apparel to make sure there are no knots tied in it (a knot implies impotence). For the same reason, a **Syrian** or **Moroccan** groom will be alert for a knotted kerchief slipped into his pocket by an ill-wisher, or a guest casually knotting a piece of string during the wedding ceremony. Even in **Scotland** couples used to make sure that they loosened any knots (in shoelaces and garters, for example) before the ceremony.

Not all knots are bad! In some cultures they play an important part in wedding traditions. A **Hindu** groom knots a ribbon around his bride's neck to confirm the marriage contract and make it indissoluble, and, in west India, the hands of a **Parsee** groom are tied with a seven-fold cord. The ancient **Carthaginians** tied the couple's thumbs together with a leather thong.

In Ancient Rome, a **pagan** bride wore a **white** wool dress to symbolise her virginity. The dress was girdled with a cord tied in a Herculean knot, designed to be loosened by the husband during the ceremony – the so-called marriage knot was released, not tied.

The word 'wedlock' comes from the Old English words *wed* (pledge) and *lac* (action), signifying a marriage vow.

Left: Grey or white horses are considered lucky for weddings. Here a Mohammedan bride in Iran's Mazanderan province rides a white horse to her wedding; she carries two candles symbolising her religion's 'lights of life' and she wears a traditional Moslem veil to obscure her face.

Right: A Malay bride with her bridesmaids. The bride is adorned with a crown of tinsel, gilded paper and flowers which often stays on exhibition for several days after the wedding.

CROWNING GLORY

All over the world, the bride's headdress is usually an elaborate affair, but each culture has its own idea of how it should look.

In the time of Solomon (973–933 BC), **Hebrew** brides wore plenty of gold or jewels in ropes around their headdresses, which cascaded down their cheeks and under the chin. In fact, in **Palestine** a bride will still wear her dowry on her head in the form of gold and silver chains, coins and ornaments, all suspended from a hat. **Mongolian** brides wear elaborate fan-shaped headdresses of silver and stones, while in **Sumatra** the headdress is made of golden embroidery and beads. In **Denmark** the traditional headdress was shaped like a horn, bearing a veil and tiara.

In northern and central **Europe**, the bride's crown might include a dramatic circle of lighted candles (though this was more often a New Year crown) and some of the **Scandinavian** bridal crowns are very elaborate, not to mention heavy

A Matyo woman in Hungary continues to wear her floral bridal crown for a year after her wedding, but in Switzerland the floral wreath suggests maidenhood and is set alight after the ceremony as a symbol of the ashes of virginity. In Normandy maidenhead is symbolised by a single white rose which the bride wears in her hair for the wedding and lays at the head of the marriage bed on her wedding night.

By the 16th century the European bride's headpiece was an elaborate concoction supported by a metal frame, piled with symbolic blossoms and including ears of wheat for fertility.

Left: This Hungarian newlywed couple are in traditional folk costume – note the bride's elaborate headdress.

Right: An Indian bridegroom in Udaipur in 1986, acknowledging traditional offerings during his procession.

to wear, because they include so much gold, or gilded silver, as well as glittering mirrors and masses of flowers, ribbons and pearls. An elaborate floral headdress with lots of coloured streamers is traditionally worn by a Lowicz bride in **Poland**.

A bride in **Ancient Rome** would have worn a flame-coloured veil under a chaplet of myrtle and vervain – her *corona nuptialis* (wedding crown) which was a symbol of triumph and fertility.

But why should women always be the decorated ones? At rural weddings in **Greece**, the groom as well as the bride wears an evergreen wreath woven with orange blossom or wild hyacinths. Well, it makes a change from the old top hat, doesn't it!

Lapel buttonholes were first made by tailors in the 1840s and the carnation soon became the favourite bloom for the groom and his men to wear. These days, white carnations or gardenias are a popular choice although, ideally, the groom should complement the bride by wearing a flower from her bouquet.

In Tudor times, flowers were strewn in the bride's path, and the custom is still remembered today in America, though it is more likely that a small bridesmaid will walk ahead of the bride, carrying a basketful of petals without scattering them.

WELL GROOMED

The regulation 'uniform' of the modern bridegroom and his party is quite a recent fashion and there was a time, not long ago, when bridegrooms dressed much more colourfully. In the early 1860s society bridegrooms wore **frock-coats** in claret, mulberry or blue. These had velvet collars and were worn over single-breasted white or patterned **waistcoats**, and doeskin **trousers** in pale drab or lavender. The male guests were just as brightly dressed, unless the groom was a clergyman in which case black or dark green coats were more suitable. **Top hats** were typical, and could be blue, grey, black or white. So, for at least three decades, it was the men who contributed the colour to weddings, as brides tended to favour pale colours.

The dark blue or black **morning coat** began to come into fashion in the 1880s. This was cut away from the waist and fell in tails at the back to just above the knee. By the time of the First World War, this style had become a 'uniform' at tradesmen's weddings, but the frock-coat remained popular among high-society grooms and their men.

Introduced in the 1880s, the **lounge suit** was a favourite at the weddings of the working class because it was so affordable. It was often worn with a **billycock hat, gloves** and a **buttonhole**, and this style increased in popularity up to the Second World War.

During the war, of course, many bridegrooms wore their service uniforms, and the Royal Navy allowed able-seamen to add white wedding ribbons worn as streamers on the chest of the uniform.

Left: Traditional Dutch wedding outfits – the groom's dress-pantaloons are typical of Old Holland, and his outfit is probably as colourful as the bride's.

Right: Late Victorian wedding group – the men are in dark morning-coats (fashionable since the 1880s) with white carnation buttonholes.

By the 1960s, some men still wore morning dress – usually hired – or dark lounge suits, but in the 1970s grooms at last broke the mould and became more colourful again. At many registry office weddings flamboyancy was the name of the game and pop stars were renowned for their weird and wonderful attire.

DRESSING UP

White weddings were unusual before the 20th century. They were generally reserved for high-society brides, while lesser mortals simply wore their best clothes. In fact, the tradition of an all-white outfit for the bride is largely a Victorian invention (Queen Victoria's daughters set the precedent). At the beginning of the 19th century, the bride might have worn a white dress, but it would have been covered by a richly coloured tiny jacket or long coat. However, there was an *American* all-white wedding as early as 1800, and well before then the bride of France's Louis XII, Anne of Brittany, had a white wedding.

Wedding fashions tended to reflect everyday fashions. For example, in the 1850s society brides wore flounced dresses over bell-shaped **crinolines,** with wide sleeves and a lowish neckline. In the following decade they wore full-skirted silk taffeta dresses over crinoline petticoats which fell fairly straight at the front and spread out behind. The close-fitting bodice had a high, plain, round neckline with silk fringing on the yoke, and the sleeves were long and fitted. Towards the end of that decade, white 'book-muslin' was more in

In Europe, it was often the custom to wear national or regional costume, and in Poland brides wore gaily striped skirts and the men striped trousers. It could be said that Hungarian brides were kept well and truly 'under wraps' – they traditionally wore up to 20 petticoats under their wedding clothes!

favour than heavy satins and silks and the style included a generous **train** with 'puffings' divided by lace sections. The royal princesses soon set a fashion for bridal dresses elaborately swagged and festooned with wreaths of flowers and swathes of tulle and lace.

In the 1880s, the discovery of aniline dyes meant that brides could at last be more adventurous. The pastels of the previous decades gave way to a host of glorious shades and purple satin, bronze taffeta and claret-coloured velvet were popular choices, although some brides still preferred white.

The **Edwardians** were more frivolous than the Victorians and favoured softer styles with the frothiness of lace and chiffon, soft drapes of velvet and ninon over severe corsets. Although ivory remained a favourite colour, it was in a mixture of fabrics in the dress. By about 1912, pale grey embroidered with seed pearls was the fashion for bridal gowns and occasionally brides wore tailored wedding suits with lacy blouses rather than dresses. They also chose **hats** rather than wedding veils, and the hats grew larger and larger up until the First World War.

In 1886 the canonical law changed and weddings could take place in the afternoon. It followed that many brides chose to marry in their going-away outfits and during the 1890s the typical wedding dress had fashionable leg-of-mutton sleeves and a tightly sashed waist.

In Britain, veils did not come into favour until the 19th century. Before then, brides wore flowers in their hair, or hats or caps.

A Serbian bride in Yugoslavia traditionally hid behind a gorgeous, elaborate, full-length veil for the whole of her wedding day – absolutely no one was to see her unveiled. Sometimes the veil was a family heirloom handed down for several generations, or else the girl would have made it herself over a period of several years.

At an Islamic wedding, the bride's veil completely covers her from head to toe and in some cases the bridegroom (who wears a white silk shawl draped over his head and shoulders) might not have seen her at all before the wedding and will have no idea what her face looks like until the celebrations are over. His bride is likely to wear a red tunic and ruffled trousers under the veil.

The war saw brides in plainly cut going-away **suits** with wide collars, set off by gloves and tidy round hats. Hemlines began to rise, though they dropped back to the ankles after the war. In the 1920s, wedding dresses became shorter again and were in afternoon-dress style rather than evening fashions. Pastels were as common as white and cream, but the real favourites were blues, pinks and peaches.

In the 1930s, the style swung to 'Hollywood romantic' on the one hand, and elegantly simple evening dresses on the other. The medieval look became popular, as did flowery garden-party chiffons with full-length skirts worn with matching long-sleeved jackets. Beribboned Dolly Varden straw hats and perky little cloches were the fashionable headwear. Later in the decade, the sweetheart neckline was introduced with padded shoulders, and long sleeves ending in V-shapes over the back of the hand. White came firmly back into fashion – a cold, pure white satin often with a flower pattern woven into the material. However, at less formal weddings brides still wore coloured dresses.

Just after the Second World War a few women made their wedding petticoats and nightdresses from the parachute silk that was readily available – in lime or orange as well as white!

The Second World War brought the cold draught of **utility**, but many brides borrowed and scraped to wed in long white dresses. Others, however, preferred tidy, tailored suits with padded shoulders and semi-fitted waists. It was fashionable to pin a corsage of flowers to the lapel and wear a hat perched at a jaunty angle with a wisp of a veil. Servicewomen began to follow the example of their male counterparts and marry in uniform.

After the war, white weddings made a comeback in spite of clothes **rationing** and many brides stitched their own dresses in the 'New Look'. Alternatively, as this practice began in the post-war years, a woman could hire her dress.

Thereafter, wedding dresses vaguely followed the general fashions of the day. Short-jacketed suits or ballerina-length wedding dresses were worn for a while in the 1950s, and with the 60s came the mini-skirted dress and coat. However, it was still common for the bride to wear an imitation of a historical style, be it Victorian, Regency or Edwardian.

In the 1970s, many brides chose traditional long white dresses, but others enjoyed themselves in colourful kaftans, 'antique' dresses bought secondhand, flower-printed long dresses and the like. The traditional outfits, complete with veils and trains, were very often hired for the day.

There are numerous superstitions surrounding a Western bride's wedding clothes. Above all, everything she wears must be **new** (to symbolise her new life), including pins and underwear, except the traditional 'something old' or 'something borrowed' which might be a family veil, perhaps, or an old pair of shoes.

The bride should never make her own dress, nor should she try on the complete outfit too soon and certainly not in front of a **mirror** – it's the old superstition about anticipation jeopardising the future. She should wait until the last moment

Left: A Scottish piper signals the completion of the church formalities at the wedding of Mr Kenneth G. Garner-Smith (of the Seaforth Highlanders) and his bride Mary Jean (née Macdonald) in London in 1933.

Right: Cutting the cake at a wartime wedding (1940).

before leaving for the ceremony, and only then can she look at herself in the mirror – but she must make sure the outfit is incomplete.

During fittings for the dress, she should never wear the whole ensemble but try on only separate parts of it. Ideally the **dressmaker** should not complete her work until the very last moment, perhaps by employing the trick of leaving a few stitches unsewn along the hem until just before the bride leaves home. She should never whistle while working on the dress.

Old **shoes** are tied to the carriage that takes the couple away after the wedding, and baby-shoes are considered extra lucky. More rumbustiously, shoes are sometimes thrown at the couple for good fortune (said to be even luckier if one of the pair is hit by a flying shoe, though the target might not agree!). Brides sometimes throw their right shoe rather than their bouquet after the wedding, but the principle, that the person who catches it will be next to marry, remains the same.

Bride-favours were ribbon love-knots loosely tacked to the bride's dress so that they could easily be pulled off during the festivities by young men, who wore them as lucky tokens in their hats in the 16th and 17th centuries. Snatched **garters** then took the place of ribbon favours – after they had been removed from the bride following the ceremony young men would race for them. The winner of the race wore the garter in his hat for good luck.

At one time the bride's garter was snatched off actually in the church as soon as the vows had been taken, or just outside it immediately after the ceremony. The garter was in the form of a ribbon loosely tied below the knee and she would helpfully lift her skirt so that it could be pulled off.

Other 'bride prizes' which were raced for included a key to her bedchamber, bottles of rum or whisky, bride-cakes or, in the north of England, savoury cabbage!

Knives have played their part in wedding outfits, too. From at least the late Middle Ages until the 18th century, a bride would attach to her girdle a specially made pair of knives held in a single sheath to symbolise that she was the new mistress of a new household.

Greek brides carry a **sugarlump** in their glove to ensure sweetness in the marriage.

In 1990, Japanese designer Asami Kobayashi was commissioned by the precious-metals group Johnson Matthey to make a dress of very thin platinum foil, lined with Japanese paper and then shredded into threads for weaving. It is worth £300 000.

The world's longest wedding-dress train measured just over 97ft 7in (29.8m) and was made by Margaret Riley of Thurnby Lodge, Leicester for the blessing of the marriage of Diane and Steven Reid in Thurmaston, Leicester on 6th May, 1990.

Not so long ago, wedding-veil embroiderers would work into the veil a long, fair hair from some woman's head. If the hair remained intact the marriage would be long and happy. However, if it broke at the beginning of the weaving, the wife would die early, or, if it broke near the end, the husband would be the one to die prematurely.

A Yorkshire bride, if she was a virgin, might have worn a garter made of straw to ensure her fertility. She went secretly to the fields on a Friday night before the wedding and took from the stacks one wheat straw for every son she hoped for and one oat straw for every daughter. She plaited them into a garter and wore it until the following Monday morning, making sure that her future husband knew nothing about it. If she was not a virgin, the weaving of a straw garter put all her future children at great risk.

> *Something old, something new,*
> *Something borrowed, something blue,*
> *And a sixpence in her shoe.*

Coins in the shoe are thought to ensure future wealth. In Sweden, it is two coins – one of silver and one of gold – and in America a gold dollar is used.

The lucky **horseshoe** is actually another fertility charm, with many lunar associations. The luckiest is from the near (left) hind foot of a grey mare.

BRIDESMAIDS

In England, it was the wedding of Princess Alexandra in 1863 that started a wave of fashion for having lots of **bridesmaids**, dressed rather like the bride in that they wore white dresses and veils and were bedecked with blossoms. By the 1870s, the bride might have been in white but her bridesmaids were a colourful contrast, wearing pastel-coloured dresses trimmed with darker colours and ribbons, and elaborately feathered straw hats.

In the 1880s it became popular to have very young **pageboys** as well as bridesmaids. The little boys generally wore military uniform while the girls' outfits once again imitated the bride's. By Edwardian times, the young bridesmaids' bonnets were as big as those of the older ones.

At the turn of the century, day-dress styles and suits were popular among adult bridesmaids, but by the 1920s, bonnets had been replaced by fashionable cloches. In the 1930s they donned richly coloured velvet 'medieval' dresses which they wore with long gloves, capes and lace-trimmed Juliet caps, while the little girls wore lots of tiered frills in pastel shades.

During the Second World War it was uncommon to have bridesmaids, but they came back after the war during the boom in **home dressmaking**. They usually wore long-skirted dresses, though still in daywear style, but as rationing vanished (1953) their hems had moved up to mid-calf and the popular style was more like a cocktail gown than a day-dress, with matching gloves and peep-toe shoes.

In the 1960s, bridesmaid outfits often had a historical theme, but some girls favoured the fashionable short styles in apricot, peach or white. A decade later they were more likely to wear full-length flowery dresses in Laura Ashley prints with floppy hats.

The day of the bridesmaid now seems to be almost over. Her role has dwindled, except at lavish royal weddings where the bride is often attended by several very young bridesmaids and pages under the care of an older bridesmaid.

ROYAL BRIDES

Royal partnerships, by tradition, are essentially diplomatic alliances – marriages between nations or royal houses as much as the marriage of a man and a woman. It is hardly surprising, then, that some kings of the past have looked to mistresses when the marital match was less than personally satisfying. In some cases the bride was still a child, or was physically unattractive, even repugnant, to her husband. Some royal brides and their grooms couldn't even understand a word of each other's language!

> *A princely marriage is the brilliant edition of a universal fact and as such it rivets mankind.*
>
> Walter Bagehot

> *A marriage begins by joining man and wife together, but this relationship between two people, however deep at the time, needs to develop and mature with the passing years. For that it must be held firm in the web of family relationships between parents and children, between grandparents and grandchildren, between cousins, aunts and uncles.*
>
> Her Majesty Queen Elizabeth on her silver wedding anniversary, 1972

Every schoolchild knows that King
Henry VIII had six wives – but not all at
the same time, of course. It was partly his
insistence on changing wives (by divorce or
decapitation) that led to the independence of
the Church of England from the Roman
Catholic Church. Mary Queen of Scots, the
second most-wed monarch, was married
three times as regnant, and Henry VIII's sixth
wife, Catherine of Parr, outlived him and was
four times married as Queen Consort.

From the Middle Ages up to Queen Victoria's
marriage (1840), royal weddings were private
occasions traditionally held in the late evening by
candlelight (much like those of Ancient Greece
and Rome). It was not until the 20th century that
they were regularly held at **Westminster Abbey**.
Although the first royal wedding on record there
was that of Henry I to Matilda, daughter of the
King of Scotland, in 1100, and the second that of
Prince Edmund 'Crouchback', Earl of Lancaster,
to Aveline, daughter of the Count of Albemarle,
in 1269, the third was not until 1919. In that year,
Princess Patricia of Connaught married Commander the Hon Alexander Ramsay. The **Chapel
Royal** at St James's was a popular venue, as were
the **Queen's Chapel** in Whitehall and **St
George's Chapel** at Windsor.

Silver was the traditional colour for royal brides
until Victoria set a fashion for white. Victoria's
grandmother, **Princess Charlotte** of Mecklen-
burg-Strelitz, wore silver brocade with flowers
woven into it in three types of gold thread for her
wedding to **George III** in 1761. The dress was set
off by a long, ermine-edged purple train and a
small velvet cap decked with diamonds. Five years
later, the Danish **Princess Sophia Magdalena**
wore silver-and-white brocade for her wedding to
King Gustavus III of Sweden and, until the end
of the 18th century, royal bridegrooms were
resplendent in silver cloth with velvet
overmantles, trains, silk stockings and rosetted
satin shoes.

It is said that the future **George IV** was so
repelled at the sight of his bride, **Princess Caroline** of Brunswick, that he could only face his wed-

ding ceremony in an alcoholic haze. The physical
distaste was mutual – Caroline found 'Prinny'
equally unattractive and, after their marriage in
1795, they lived apart.

Princess Caroline's net wedding dress was heavily embroidered in silver, with an overall effect of a
lattice pattern bedecked with bells. The neckline
was low and the elbow-length sleeves were ruffled.
Her train was of silver tissue and she wore a crimson velvet mantle trimmed with ermine. She wore
her hair loose, falling over her shoulders as a symbol of her virginity, and she eschewed the fashion
for ostrich feathers on a diamond bandeau, wearing instead a small, jewelled crown. However, the
official painting of the marriage shows her in a different outfit altogether.

Despite their mutual abhorrence, the Prince
Regent and Caroline did have a child, but only
one. Their daughter, **Princess Charlotte**, married
Prince Leopold of Saxe-Coburg-Saalfeld in
1816, and she also wore silver for the wedding.
Her high-waisted dress was of white silk net
embroidered with silver flowers, leaves and shells

The only double royal wedding in
British history took place in 1818 when
Edward, Duke of Kent (who would later
become father to Queen Victoria), married
Mary Victoria, Dowager Princess of Saxe-
Meiningen, while his brother, William, Duke
of Clarence (later William IV), married
Princess Adelaide, also of Saxe-Meiningen.
Both dukes had previously been involved with
mistresses – the Irish actress, Dorothea Bland,
had already given birth to 10 illegitimate
children by William, and Edward had lived
with Madame de St Laurent for 27 years.
Parliament, however, was not impressed –
with Princess Charlotte dead there was no
heir and the line of succession was in
jeopardy. Finally, following some financial
inducements, the princes were coerced into
suitable marriages.

The weddings took place in the brides'
homeland, but there was a second joint
ceremony at the Dutch House in Kew.

over a silver underskirt and her silver-tissue train was edged with a deep frill. She wore her hair up, with a wreath of roses. However, she died in childbirth the following year.

Queen Victoria's wedding broke with royal tradition in many respects. She had hoped for a quiet ceremony at Buckingham Palace but it became a very public occasion, and it took place in broad daylight rather than at night. She married for love, having proposed to **Prince Albert** of Saxe-Coburg-Gotha with all the nervousness of a shy girl, three years after they had first met. At their wedding a year later, in 1840, they were both only 20 years old.

The Bridal Morn, engraving by S.W. Reynolds drawn by F. Lock. Queen Victoria and Prince Albert returning from their wedding ceremony on 10th February, 1840; her white satin dress has a deep flounce of Honiton lace.

They married in the Chapel Royal, St James's Palace, on a day of terrible February weather with heavy rain and gusty gales. There were 12 bridesmaids (each one was the eldest daughter of a peer, as was the tradition) wearing white dresses trimmed with roses, all designed by the Queen herself. The bride wore white rather than silver – the simple, low-necked dress was of white satin with a deep flounce of Honiton lace and a train 18ft (5.5m) long. Her short lace veil was held in place by a coronet of orange blossom (the same veil was laid over her face after she died in 1901).

Prince Albert wore the scarlet and white uniform of a British field marshal and gave the 12 bridesmaids brooches in the shape of an eagle (his own crest) set with pearls and turquoise. The wedding banquet at Buckingham Palace included a cake with a 9ft (2.7m) circumference, weighing 300lb (136kg) and costing 100 guineas, patriotically decorated with a figure of Britannia with cupids at her feet.

Victoria's wedding was before the age of **photographs**, but only just, and all her children's weddings were captured on film and kept in her family photograph album. Her daughters' wedding outfits naturally set fashion trends and were copied by brides all over the country – and indeed throughout the British Empire. It was they who set the trend for all-white weddings.

The Queen's eldest daughter, **Princess Vicky**, married **Prince Frederick William** of Prussia in the Chapel Royal at St James's Palace on a blustery, overcast day in 1858. It was three years later that the whole nation was plunged into deep mourning at the sudden death of Prince Albert (Victoria was a widow for 50 years), and it was still in mourning at the time of the marriage of Vicky's sister, **Princess Alice**, to **Prince Louis** of Hesse in 1862. Before his death, Prince Albert had personally designed the veil for Alice's wedding and she wore it with a wreath of orange blossom while the same flowers decorated the hem of her simple white lace crinoline dress. All the female guests wore the mourning colours of purple and grey and the men, including the bridegroom, wore black tailcoats, grey trousers and white waistcoats. The Queen herself was in black. The ceremony took place very privately in the dining-room at Osborne House on the Isle of Wight.

The following year, '**Bertie**' (Edward, Prince of Wales, the Queen's eldest son and heir) married **Princess Alexandra** of Denmark in St George's Chapel at Windsor. The bride wore white satin and tulle, swathed with orange blossom and myrtle, and the eight bridesmaids were in white tulle bedecked with roses, shamrocks and heather, with the same combination of flowers forming the wreaths that secured their veils. The bridegroom wore a general's scarlet tunic under his blue velvet Knight of the Garter mantle, complete with the mantle's traditional tasselled cord which, according to the Hon Sir George Bellew, former Garter King of Arms, is extremely difficult to tie correctly. The Queen was still in deepest mourning for Prince Albert and secreted herself in Queen Catherine of Aragon's closet during the ceremony so that she could watch without being seen.

Princess Louise, the fourth daughter of Queen Victoria, wore a bustle under a dress festooned with flowers near the hem and on the borders of the bodice when she married the **Marquess of Lorne** at St George's Chapel in 1871. Three years later **Prince Alfred**, Duke of Edinburgh, married **Grand Duchess Marie** of Russia at the romantic Winter Palace in St Petersburg, Russia, but the **Duke of Connaught** chose Windsor for his marriage to **Princess Louise Margaret** of Prussia, in 1879.

In contrast to these high-society weddings, Queen Victoria's youngest child, **Princess 'Baby' Beatrice**, chose to marry **Prince Henry** of Battenberg in the small parish church of St Mildred, in Whippingham, near Osborne on the Isle of Wight. Queen Victoria, who fondly described it as a 'village wedding', gave the bride away herself. The Princess's face was virtually framed with flowers, and they lavishly decorated the lacy neckline of her dress, almost weighing her down while more flowers mingled with the diamond stars of her headdress.

Queen Victoria's grandson, **Prince Albert Victor** (nicknamed Eddy), firmly believed in 'having a good time'. However, this gave rise to increasingly outrageous rumours which included stories that he had an illegitimate child by a prostitute, indulged in homosexual affairs, and was connected with the notorious Jack the Ripper murders. It was hoped that his proposed marriage to

Princess Louise (Queen Victoria's daughter) and her new husband, the Marquess of Lorne, after their Windsor wedding in 1871. Slippers are being thrown for good luck.

Princess Victoria Mary of Teck would stabilise him, but it was not to be. In 1892, six weeks before the planned wedding, he caught 'flu and died.

In due course, **Princess Mary** married his younger brother, **Prince George**, Duke of York (later King George V), in St James's Chapel Royal. It was a hot July day and a very public and popular event – St James's Park was bursting with good-natured crowds cheering the procession of carriages. The bridegroom wore naval uniform while the bride, attended by five little bridesmaids and five adult ones, wore satin brocade embroidered with patriotic silver roses, thistles and shamrocks

and festooned with orange blossom. At her home, White Lodge, the almond trees caught the mood of jubilation and bore a heavy crop of nuts – promising a fruitful marriage (which it was).

In 1922, the couple's daughter, **Princess Mary**, married **Henry, Viscount Lascelles**, with plenty of ceremony and splash, arriving at Westminster Abbey in the Irish state coach. The bride reverted to the royal tradition of silver rather than white, with an elegant gown of silver lamé under a mist of fine ivory marquisette net embroidered with silver roses, thousands of seed pearls and crystals in a trellis design. The white duchess satin train was

After the First World War, a royal wedding was just the tonic Britain needed. The marriage, in 1919, was that of Queen Victoria's granddaughter, Princess Patricia of Connaught, and Commander the Hon Alexander Ramsey. Previously, the Princess had rejected several marriage proposals, including those from King Alfonso of Spain and Grand Duke Cyril of Russia. Her father was Governor-General of Canada and she became his official hostess there following the death of her mother. She was greatly loved and known affectionately as 'Princess Pat'.

full and very long, heavily embroidered with silver emblems, pearls and diamonds, and bordered with deep cascades of Honiton lace. It was held at the shoulders with embroidered pearl-and-crystal clasps and she wore two ropes of pearls strung on silver cords as a girdle, with a trailing bunch of silver-stemmed orange blossom at her waist. Her long veil was edged with yet more pearls and was held in place by three narrow circlets of orange blossom.

The following year saw the marriage of **Lady Elizabeth Bowes-Lyon** (now the Queen Mother) to the **Duke of York**, who was destined to become King George VI. On 26th April, a wet, overcast day, she travelled to Westminster Abbey in a maroon-and-gold landau drawn by four grey horses and, as if by magic, the sun came out just as she arrived. She was elegantly dressed in a simple, narrow gown of ivory silk crêpe-moire embroidered with pearls, little iridiscent white beads and bands of silver lamé. She borrowed a long, floating veil of point-de-Flandres lace from her mother-in-law, Queen Mary, and held it in place with a slender circlet of myrtle leaves clamped fashionably low on her forehead, with white roses and orangeblossom over each ear. Before the service, she placed her bouquet of white roses on the tomb of the Unknown Soldier.

The wedding of the **Duke of Windsor**, the exiled brother of King George VI, was an entirely different affair. In 1937, his marriage to **Mrs Wallis Simpson** took place at the Château de Cande,

Tours, with a civil ceremony followed by a religious one in the music room – with an English priest (Rev R Anderson Jardine) from St Paul's, Darlington, officiating. It was a warm, sunny day and Mrs Simpson wore a long gown of pale blue crêpe satin with a small veiled hat with matching blue feathers.

Then came the Second World War and all its traumas, but once again there was a royal wedding to lift the nation's heart after the war was over. In 1947, **Princess Elizabeth** married **Lieutenant Philip Mountbatten, RN** (previously Prince Philip of Greece), whom she had first met when she was only 13 years old. Just like any other bride in that time of rationing, the future Queen saved up her clothes coupons, though she was granted some extra ones by the government for such a public occasion.

The Westminster Abbey wedding took place on a cold, wet, windy day – 20th November, 1947. The bridegroom wore his naval uniform, the two pageboys were in kilts, and the eight bridesmaids wore spangled fluffy-looking white tulle, long white gloves and floral headdresses. The bride was radiant in a Norman Hartnell gown with a fitted bodice, sweetheart neckline, padded shoulders and long, slightly flared skirts of ivory satin which were scattered with embroidered garlands of York roses. A tiara held her veil in place and she carried a bouquet which had almost failed to arrive –it couldn't be found because someone had considerately put it in the fridge to keep it fresh!

The wedding gifts came from all over the world and many were magnificent, but perhaps the most original were an ostrich-feather cape from South Africa's ostrich farmers, 1000 Montevidean blankets to be distributed to poor London children, a necklace of 96 rubies from Burma and, most touching of all, a lacy shawl handknitted by Mahatma Gandhi.

In 1972, on the 25th anniversary of the marriage of the Queen and Prince Philip, 100 other couples who had wedded on that day in 1947 came to Westminster Abbey to share a special service with the royal couple.

The Duke of York (later King George VI) and his bride, the former Lady Elizabeth Bowes-Lyon (now the Queen Mother) on their wedding day, 26th April, 1923.

When the limousine carrying the newly-married Princess Margaret and her husband, Antony Armstrong-Jones, slowed to a walking pace because of the surrounding crowd, someone scratched a heart into the maroon paintwork.

The 1960s and 70s saw a spate of royal weddings. On 6th May, 1960, **Princess Margaret** married **Antony Armstrong-Jones**, and she too wore a Hartnell dress. It was made from 30 yards (27.4m) of finest white silk organza fashioned into a fitted V-necked bodice which flared out into a full skirt in 12 panels and formed a cloudy train. Her hair was swept up with a diamond tiara holding the long, full veil of white silk tulle and organza. Her bouquet was made up of stephanotis and orchids. The dresses of the eight young bridesmaids were white organza trimmed with lace and were copies of the Princess' first ballgown – the one her father loved to see her wear.

Princess Margaret was married in Westminster Abbey, but the following year the **Duke of Kent** married **Katharine Worsley** of Hovingham Hall at York Minster, on a fickle June day with bright sunshine alternating with heavy bursts of rain. The bride's dress, designed by John Cavanagh, was made from 237 yards (216.7m) of French white silk gauze – the very full train was 15ft (4.6m) long. The eight bridesmaids were in long white organdie dresses with cream and yellow rosebuds in their hair, and there were three little pageboys in kneebreeches.

Another 1960s wedding was that of **Princess Alexandra** to the **Hon Angus Ogilvy**. They married in 1963 at Westminster Abbey and the bride wore a Cavanagh design – a plain, classic style made from 80 yards (73m) of magnolia French lace appliquéd on white tulle and hand-embroidered with thousands of gold paillettes so that it shimmered subtly. Her train was 21ft (6.4m) long and was worn as a veil – that is, from the head rather than the shoulders or waist. She also wore Queen Charlotte's antique veil, as Princess Patricia had in 1919, and its acorn pattern was taken up on her gown. The two pageboys wore

kilts while the five bridesmaids were in long dresses of pale cream ziberline with wide trumpet sleeves.

In 1972 **Prince Richard**, Duke of Gloucester, married **Birgitte van Deurs** of Denmark at St Andrew's church near Barwell Manor; and in 1978 **Prince Michael** of Kent married **Marie-Christine von Reibnitz** in Vienna. However, the major royal wedding of the time was that of **Princess Anne** and **Captain Mark Phillips**, on 14th November, 1973. It was another Abbey wedding and was the first royal wedding to be seen in colour on television, with live broadcasts to Europe, the United States and even Japan, and an estimated audience of about 530 million people. The dress, designed by Maureen Baker (of Susan Small Ltd), was in ivory, in a princess-line style with a fitted pintuck bodice, and a semi-full skirt which broadened into a semi-circular train. Seed pearls, small mirror jewels and silver embroidery enhanced the outfit, and over her upswept hair she wore her grandmother's diamond tiara, modelled on a Romanian peasant's headdress. Her bouquet included myrtle from the bush grown from a sprig in Queen Victoria's wedding bouquet. **Lady Sarah Armstrong-Jones** (Princess Margaret's daughter) was the only bridesmaid.

For the record, Princess Anne's wedding cake weighed 145lb (65.8kg) and was baked by Warrant Officer David Dodd of the Army Catering Corps, who used 12½lb (5.7kg) of flour, 84 eggs, 16lb (7.3kg) of marzipan and two bottles of brandy.

The fairytale royal wedding of the century was surely that of **Prince Charles**, Prince of Wales, to **Lady Diana Spencer** on 29th July, 1981. The Prince, as it happened, had been present at his future wife's *christening* but their first 'real' meeting took place in a ploughed field during a shoot many years later, when he was a friend of Diana's elder sister, Sarah. The romance grew, in spite of the pitiless pursuit by the press, though Prince Charles was heard to say, shortly before his engagement to Diana was announced: 'I must take up the Muslim religion – and have lots of wives.' The huge sapphire engagement ring, from Garrards, was surrounded by 14 large diamonds.

The royal wedding became a major media event. Half a million people crowded into Hyde

Park for pre-wedding fireworks set to Handel's *Water Music*, and more than 500 million worldwide watched live television broadcasts of the wedding itself, which was held at St Paul's Cathedral – it can accommodate 2500 guests whereas Westminster Abbey only takes about 1800. The Cathedral was lavishly decorated with pink and purple flowers.

Lady Diana and her father, the 8th Earl Spencer (former Equerry to the Queen), rode to the Cathedral in the Glass Coach, drawn by two Windsor greys (Lady Penelope and St David) driven by senior coachman Richard Boland. They arrived only one minute late.

The gorgeous, romantic, billowing wedding dress was designed by David and Elizabeth Emanuel, who claimed to have been inspired by watching old films on television. It was made of ivory silk, adorned with Carrickmacross lace which had belonged to Queen Mary and the puff sleeves had deep lace cuffs. David Emanuel stitched a tiny good-luck charm in the shape of a gold horseshoe studded with diamonds to the hem. The net veil was held in place by the Iveagh family tiara. Prince Charles wore his naval uniform and the bridesmaids, in the charge of **Lady Sarah Armstrong-Jones**, wore golden-yellow sashes to match the colour of the Mountbatten roses in the bride's bouquet. These roses were a gift from the Worshipful Company of Gardeners – they were intended as a gesture to the importance of the late Lord Mountbatten in Prince Charles' life.

The bouquet included:
    Mountbatten roses
    Stephanotis
    White freesias
    Lily-of-the-valley
    Odontoglossum orchids
    Ivy leaves
    Myrtle and veronica sprigs

After the wedding ceremony itself, the most celebrated event was the 'Balcony Kiss' which the couple exchanged to the delight of the crowds massed below the Buckingham Palace balcony.

The wedding night was spent at Broadlands and it is rumoured that the new Princess slept-in the following morning while her husband rose early, relished a substantial country-house breakfast and went fishing on the Test.

A Royal Love Story was the title of a film based on the romance of Prince Charles and Lady Diana, with Catherine Oxenburg starring as the girl with the becoming blush.

The famous kiss: Prince Charles and his princess, Diana, on the Buckingham Palace balcony after their wedding on 29th July, 1981.

The most recent royal wedding was that of **Prince Andrew** and **Miss Sarah Ferguson**. Her father, Ronnie Ferguson, was polo manager to Andrew's brother, the Prince of Wales, and the couple are said to have met on a polo field. Sarah's engagement ring, which cost £25 000 before it was even set, also came from Garrards and was an enormous cabuchon ruby surrounded by ten diamonds.

The wedding took place almost exactly five years after that of Charles and Diana, on 23rd July, 1986, and was at Westminster Abbey – the ninth royal wedding in the Abbey during this century. Only an hour before the ceremony, the Queen created Andrew the 14th Duke of York, so that Sarah became Duchess of York when they married. Her dress was a Lindka Ceirach design made of duchess satin, and a little blue bow had been stitched to the underskirts for luck. The colour theme for the flowers was peach.

The Royal Family always sits on the righthand side of the church, regardless of whether it is the marriage of a royal son or a royal daughter. The rule for lesser mortals is that the bridegroom's family and guests sit on the right, and those of the bride on the left.

Queen Aishwarya of Nepal is a rather colourful character who has been described as 'a cross between Imelda Marcos of the Philippines and the late Elena Ceausescu of Romania'. She is a member of the Rana clan (which governed Nepal for a century up to 1951) and is as outspoken and forceful as her husband, King Birenda, is introverted and amenable. In 1990, she was supposedly locked in her bedroom at their palace in Kathmandu for throwing a teapot at his head! There are rumours about the real power behind the throne.

According to a humorous *Daily Mirror* article published a few years ago, the future wife of Prince Hiro, Crown Prince of Japan, would have to be younger than him, and shorter when she stood in high heels; she must never have worked in an office under a boss, and her father must never have had extramarital relationships.

On 29th June, 1990, Prince Aya, second in line to the Japanese Chrysanthemum Throne, married Kiko Kawashima – a commoner and, as such, only the second to marry into the royal family. Prior to the wedding she was a psychology student but is now referred to as a *hakoirimusume* ('daughter kept in a box'). 'Za Royaru Weddingu' was a major media event covered by six television channels, each of which spent more than 500 million yen (£1.88 million) to secure transmission rights. Ninety-eight million viewers tuned-in to the coverage, which began at 6.30 am as the bride left her family home, bowing to her parents and younger brothers before being taken to the Imperial Palace in a black limousine.

It took three and a half hours to squeeze the bride into the 12 layers of her traditional imperial wedding kimono, weighing about 30lb (13.6kg), and the wig of long, lacquered hair which almost reached her ankles. It was rumoured that, for three days before, the poor girl had existed on a non-liquid diet to avoid having to unwrap the kimono for a call of nature. For those who want to know, the bride's favourite drink is iced apple tea with a spoonful of marmalade.

The ceremony, which took place in the Kashikodokoro Imperial Shrine at the palace, began at 10 am – and lasted only 15 minutes. By tradition there was no confetti, no smiling and certainly no kissing (displays of emotion are not acceptable).

STAR WARS

Marriage and love is never out of fashion in Holly-wood – in fact it is almost an addiction. Here are some major addicts, starting with the most-married:

8 TIMES

Mickey Rooney: Ava Gardner 1942, Betty Jane Rase 1944, Martha Vickers 1949, Elaine Mahuken 1952, Barbara Thomason 1958, Margaret Lane 1966, Carolyn Hackett 1969, Jan Chamberlain 1975.

Lana Turner: bandleader Artie Shaw 1940, res-taurateur Stephen Crane, twice (1942 and 1943), baseball team owner Bob Topping 1948, actor Lex Barker (Tarzan) 1953, rancher Fred May 1960, writer Robert Eaton 1965 (ten years her junior), hypnotist Ronald Dante for a few months in 1969 – and at least seven famous lov-ers including Howard Hughes, Tyrone Power and the gangster Johnny Stompanato.

7 TIMES

Elizabeth Taylor: hotel heir Nicky Hilton 1950, actor Michael Wilding 1952, producer Mike Todd 1957, singer Eddie Fisher 1959, actor Richard Burton, twice (1964 and briefly in 1975), John Warner 1976.

6 TIMES

Gloria Swanson: Wallace Beery 1916, Herbert Somborn 1919, Henri de la Falaise 1925, Michael Farmer 1931, William Davey 1945, William Dufty 1976 – and plenty of lovers in between, including the father of future Presi-dent Kennedy.

5 TIMES

Richard Burton: Sybil Williams 1949, Elizabeth Taylor 1964 and 1975, Susan Hunt 1976, Sally Hay 1983.

Henry Fonda: Margaret Sullavan 1931, Frances Brokaw 1936, Susan Blanchard 1950, Alfreda Franchetti 1957, Shirlee Adams 1965.

Clark Gable: Josephine Dillon 1924, Rhea Langham 1930, Carole Lombard 1939, Sylvia Hawkes 1949, Kay Spreckles 1955 – and plenty of lovers.

Judy Garland: bandleader David Rose 1941, director Vincente Minnelli 1945, producer Sid Luft 1952, Mark Herron 1965, nightclub mana-ger Mickey Deans 1969 – and lovers Tyrone Power and Joseph L Mankiewicz.

Cary Grant: Virginia Cherrill 1933, Barbara Hutton 1942, Betsy Drake 1949, Dyan Cannon 1965, Barbara Harris 1981.

Rita Hayworth: Edward Judson 1937, Orson Welles 1943, Prince Aly Khan 1949, Dick Haymes 1953, James Hill 1958.

Veronica Lake: John Detlie 1940, Andre de Toth 1944, Joseph McCarthy 1955, Ron House 1962, and for a few months in 1972 an English naval captain.

Ginger Rogers: dancer Jack Culpepper 1929, film star Lew Ayres 1934, marine private Jack Briggs 1943, actor Jacques Bergerac 1953 (20 years her junior), actor William Marshall 1961. Companion since about 1976, Greek actor and dancer George Pau, 40 years her junior. And various paramours – the ubiquitous Howard Hughes among others.

George C Scott: Carolyn Hughes 1950, Patricia Reed, Colleen Dewhurst twice (1960, 1967), Trish van Devere 1972.

4 TIMES

Humphrey Bogart: Helen Mencken 1926, Mary Phillips 1928, Mayo Methot 1938, Lauren Bacall 1945.

Charlie Chaplin: Mildred Harris 1917, Lita Grey 1924, Paulette Goddard 1936 (though possibly not formally), Oona O'Neill 1943.

Joan Crawford: Douglas Fairbanks Jnr 1929, Franchot Tone 1935, Philip Terry 1942, Alfred Steele 1956.

Bette Davis: Harmon Nelson 1932, Arthur Farnsworth 1940, William Grant Sherry 1945, Gary Merrill 1950.

Joan Fontaine: Brian Aherne 1939, William Dozier 1946, Collier Young 1952, Alfred Wright 1964.

Al Jolson: Henrietta Keller 1906, Ethel Delmar 1922, Ruby Keeler 1928 (she later claimed it was a 'long mistake'), Erle Galbraith 1945.

Myrna Loy: Arthur Hornblower Jnr 1936, John Hertz Jnr 1942, Gene Markey 1946, Howland Sargeant 1951.

Peter Sellers: Anne Haynes 1951, Britt Eckland 1964, Miranda Quarry 1970, Lynne Frederick 1976.

SOME FAMOUS 3-TIMERS

Brigitte Bardot: Roger Vadim, Jacques Charrier, Gunther Sachs von Opel – and at least 15 lovers.

Marilyn Monroe: Jim Dougherty, Joe Di Maggio, Arthur Miller – and lovers including Howard Hughes (again!), Yves Montand and the Kennedy brothers Jack and Robert.

Jean Harlow: Charles McGrew, Paul Bern, Hal Rossen – all briefly.

Erroll Flynn also married three times and had many lovers – one of them sued him for 'statutory rape' in 1942.

The famous heart-throb **Rudolph Valentino** married twice: the first marriage, to Jean Acker, only lasted a night!

OLD FAITHFULS

In spite of film stars' reputations for many marriages, some do stay true to one spouse. They include, for example, **Bob Hope** (who married Dolores Reade in 1933) and **Charles Boyer**, who married Pat Paterson in 1934 and committed suicide two days after her death in 1978. **Marlene Dietrich** only married once, in 1924, but was separated for many years without divorcing. **Katharine Hepburn** married Ludlow Ogden Smith in 1928 – in practice the marriage only lasted a few months, and she became deeply involved with Spencer Tracey from 1942 onwards.

Greta Garbo certainly did 'want to be alone' – she failed to turn up for her wedding to co-star John Gilbert.

TELLY BELLS

Soap operas rely heavily on marriage – whenever the ratings are in danger there's nothing like a wedding to send reluctant viewers racing back to their armchairs, and there's nothing like stormy marriages and love-on-the-side to keep them glued to the set. Some shorter series use the ultimate prospect of a wedding as the peg of the whole plot (will they? won't they?) – think of *Life Without George, Brushstrokes* and *To the Manor Born,* for example. Longer-running soaps like *Dallas* and *Dynasty* add a wedding every now and then but perhaps none so over the top as the Moldavian wedding massacre scene at the end of one series of *Dynasty.*

Soap fans will no doubt be able to remember on-screen weddings in *Neighbours, Emmerdale Farm* and *Brookside* but they will have to think hard about *EastEnders.* Radio fans fare better with *The Archers* but for the most weddings of all the long-running television tale of *Coronation Street* is clearly the winner. This timeless soap celebrated its silver anniversary in 1985 and since that first episode, which was broadcast on 9th December, 1960, there have been 29 on-screen weddings, as listed below.

March 1961: The Street's first wedding – Jack and Annie Walker's daughter Joan married teetotal and vegetarian teacher Gordon Davies.

October 1961: Harry Hewitt married Concepta Riley – the reception was at Greenvale Hotel (a favourite venue) and the honeymoon at the Cresta Hotel, Port Erin.

June 1962: Christine Hardman, jilted by Joe Makinson, eloped with Colin Appleby (but he was killed four months later, adding to an alarmingly high number of accidental deaths in the Street over the years).

August 1962: Ken Barlow married Valerie Tatlock – the honeymoon was in London.

October 1963: Jerry Booth married Myra Dickinson – and it was almost a double wedding when Len Fairclough proposed to Elsie Tanner, but she turned him down.

December 1965: David Barlow and Irma Ogden married quietly in the registry office but were given a surprise reception at the Greenvale Hotel.

September 1967: Steve and Elsie Tanner married at St Stephen's Methodist Church in Warrington; the honeymoon was in Lisbon. They had parted by March . . .

May 1968: Dennis Tanner married Jenny Sutton but she spent the wedding night alone in the double bed.

July 1968: Schoolgirl Audrey Bright eloped to Gretna Green with Dickie Fleming.

July 1970: Elsie Tanner quietly married Alan Howard at the registry office; the honeymoon was in Paris.

April 1972: Ernest Bishop and Emily Nugent finally got married at Mawdesley Street Congregational Church on Easter Monday, with Ena Sharples playing the organ; after a Rovers Return reception they spent their honeymoon at Edale.

October 1973: Ken Barlow married Janet Reid at the registry office.

July 1974: Ron Cooke and Maggie Clarke married at St Mary's.

July 1975: Ray Langton married Deirdre Hunt – she had recently called off her engagement to Billy Walker.

April 1977: Len Fairclough and Rita 'Mrs Bates' Littlewood married at St Margaret's to the strains of Elgar and Wagner, but the music changed to Victor Sylvester at the Greenvale reception.

March 1978: Awkward Alf Roberts tied the knot with Renee Bradshaw at the registry office; the honeymoon was in Capri.

November 1979: Brian Tilsley and Gail Potter had a white wedding in church, and a reception at the Rovers Return.

September 1980: Arnold Swain and widowed Emily Bishop married at the registry office but in December he was exposed as a bigamist and ended up in a mental home.

May 1981: Fred Gee married Eunice Nuttall for the sake of getting the licence of the Crown & Kettle.

July 1981: Ken Barlow married Deirdre Langton at All Saints Church; the honeymoon was in Corfu.

October 1983: Binman Eddie Yeats at last married Marion ('Stardust Lil').

September 1984: Derek Wilton and Mavis Riley both jilted each other at the altar . . .

January 1985: Bill Webster married Elaine Prior.

December 1985: Widower Alf Roberts married Audrey Potter.

May 1986: Mike Baldwin married Susan Barlow at St Mary's Parish Church.

October 1986: Kevin Webster and Sally Seddon had a registry office wedding.

September 1987: Alec Gilroy married Bet Lynch in a church ceremony at St Mary's.

February 1988: Brian and Gail Tilsley married for the second time.

June 1988: Don Brennan married widow Ivy Tilsley.

November 1988: Derek Wilton finally weds Mavis Riley.

WEDDING CEREMONIES

Marriage in **Ancient Greece** was not directly associated with the state religion but people did associate it closely with domestic religious rituals and a legally wedded woman 'came into the house with gods and sacred marriage rites' (often depicted on Greek vases). There were three main stages: preparing the bride at her father's house, her move by night to her husband's home and her reception there, and finally the giving of presents on the day after the marriage. The groom's parents greeted the couple at the bride's father's door and they then had a torchlit procession, accompanied by flute players, to the hearth-altar at the heart of the husband's house. Figs, dates and other fruit were showered on the couple as they reached the altar for the marriage ceremony. Afterwards, a torch-bearing woman led them to the bridal chamber.

The **Ancient Roman** marriage was made lawful in various ways but certain ceremonies were common to all of them – betrothal, the actual wedding rites and the night-time procession of the bride to the groom's house. The main ceremony consisted of a solemn clasping of hands while the presiding *pronuba* (a matronly friend of the bride) stood between the couple with a hand on each one's shoulder. After the exchange of vows, the ceremony was completed with a sacrifice to Jupiter, perhaps with a bull being slaughtered after the groom had poured a libation on the altar fire.

High-society weddings in Ancient Rome followed the rituals of *confarreatio*. The word means 'with spelt-cake', spelt being a rather poor sort of wheat grown in mountainous areas. The bride was conducted by a group of bachelors to the Pontifex Maximus (head of the principal college of priests). Before 10 witnesses, the couple sat on an ox-yoke,

Before the 16th century, marriage ceremonies were conducted in the church porch. It was not until the 1549 Reformation (from which the Protestant Church arose) that the couple and their kin came into the body of the church.

which symbolised marriage, and shared a spelt-cake made of flour, salt and water – the forerunner of today's wedding cake. The bride was later escorted home by married men bearing gold and silver vessels. As they went, the groom scattered nuts amongst the crowd to show that he had given up his childish pursuits.

In the **Church of England** the wedding service is a solemn affair in which the bride's father 'gives away' his daughter to the groom in the presence of a priest. After, he gives a public opportunity for objections to the marriage to be voiced, or for either of the pair to withraw at the last minute, vows are exchanged. The gist of the vows is that each will love, honour, protect and be faithful to the other for life. Originally, the bride's undertaking to obey her husband came before her promise to love him, but it is no longer an obligatory part of the vows. The Church in Wales dropped the 'obey' and the 'giving away' phrases in 1975, considering that they treated brides like chattels.

The groom places the wedding ring on his bride's wedding finger (third finger of the left hand) and the priest proclaims the marriage in the eyes of God. Traditionally, the groom is then allowed to kiss his bride, but in times gone by the priest got the first kiss, as it was said to be lucky for the marriage. The couple then sign the civil register (usually in the privacy of the vestry). This act was introduced during the 19th century and completes the civil requirements of the marriage contract.

The essence of the vows in the **Roman Catholic Church** is similar to that in the Church of England except that the couple might also undertake to bring up their children according to the laws of the Church.

In the **Eastern Orthodox Church**, the bride and groom are both crowned by the priest – the groom is blessed in the names of Abraham, Isaac and Jacob, and the bride in the names of Sarah, Rebecca and Rachel. Respectively, both sets of names mean 'exalted', 'blessed' and 'fertile'.

Quaker weddings have no officiating minister or best man or bridesmaids. The couple sit next to each other at a Friends' meeting, wearing their best

Left: A Polynesian bride walking on her wedding guests: a typically fanciful 19th-century interpretation of 'strange native customs', printed in Sunday At Home, *1874.*

Right: A fashionable London wedding in 1849.

everyday clothes, and simply stand up to tell the Friends in formal words that they take each other as husband and wife. All those present sign the register as witnesses.

In a **registry office**, the ceremony is very simple and brief. The couple marry each other in the presence of witnesses before a presiding registrar, and their act is registered.

The **Jewish** ceremony centres on the *chuppah* – a symbolic marriage chamber made up of four poles decorated with flowers which support a canopy to provide privacy. The best man accompanies the groom to the chuppah and they are joined there by the rabbi, the groom's parents and the bride's mother. Last of all comes the bride, led by her father to a musical accompaniment. As soon as she steps under the canopy of the chuppah, she is considered married. The subsequent ceremony begins with the welcoming of the couple and a brief address to them, followed by benedictions and wine-drinking. The couple recite simple vows and the ring is given.

There is then a public reading of the previously agreed marriage contract, which is signed by the bride and groom, and the ceremony continues with the singing of liturgical benedictions, more wine-drinking for the couple and, finally, a closing benediction. The groom then breaks a glass before he and his bride sign the civil register and head for the wedding feast – which may last for up to a week!

The formal **Islamic** marriage ceremony is beautifully simple. In front of the invited friends and family (with no priests or officials) the parents, or the couple, announce the marriage by saying in one sentence that each agrees to marry the other – and that is that. Sometimes the marriage is formally registered to safeguard the future interests of both sides. The husband, by accepting the marriage contract, becomes financially responsible for his wife's maintenance and, although most men then settle for one wife, he is allowed to marry up to four if he can support them.

In a marriage between two followers of the **Baha'i** faith, a very simple vow is made to abide by the will of God. There may be accompanying prayers and readings, chosen by the couple, and some like to have music, singing or chanting – whatever they feel is appropriate.

A **Hindu** marriage involves far more elaborate celebrations with a large number of relations and friends. Often the ceremony lasts for several days, and is usually held in a big marquee either in the bride's home courtyard or in a large, hired wedding hall in the city. The home, rather than the temple, is the centre of worship and that is where the family priest will conduct the initial rituals of the marriage ceremony.

The ceremony itself is short and includes specific rituals, though the details vary in different communities. Before the marriage, the girl's parents promise to give their daughter away and the boy's parents confirm their acceptance of her as their son's bride. On the wedding day (or the day before) the young bride and groom-to-be each have baths, put on clean clothes and make ritual prayers asking for God's blessing. When the groom's party arrives in the bride's home town there is a welcoming ceremony and the groom is invited to dine at the bride's house.

Just before the time so carefully chosen for the marriage, the couple stand on a special decorated board, separated from each other by a curtain. The bride's maternal uncle and bridesmaids stand behind her while priests sing marriage hymns and all those present shower the couple with rice. At the appointed time, the curtain is removed and the couple exchange garlands. The bride is then given away to the groom by her father and gifts are exchanged. Cotton is tied around the couple to signify unity and they shower each other with rice. Then the groom ties a special wedding necklace around his bride's neck as a love token – it has on it two golden semicircles which represent the union of the two families.

The ceremony continues with the bride dabbing the groom's forehead with sandalwood paste and he marks hers with red powder. They then make offerings of puffed rice and ghee to the fire, after which they hold hands and go round the fire together enacting certain rituals while the priests chant mantras. Rather delightfully, the seventh and final step in this ritual is an avowal of friendship: 'I shall ever befriend you and you do the same. Never break our friendship . . .' Finally,

In Thailand, a man traditionally worked in his future father-in-law's fields for a few years to earn the right to marry his bride. He was also expected to spend at least three months as a monk, and he had to build his bride a house in her father's compound, for which the father supplied the furniture. Only when the house was complete did they go about arranging an auspicious wedding date and time.

the girl is taken to her new home, with ceremonial blessings from her elders on both sides of the family.

Sikh marriage ceremonies in India are often full of pageantry. Any well-respected Sikh (male or female) can officiate, and there is much singing, praying and blessing, with a lecture on what is expected of the couple in marriage. They signal their acceptance of those obligations by bowing. They are then garlanded and are joined by a saffron-coloured scarf for the rituals. Flower petals are scattered over them by the congregation and the husband is asked to love and respect his wife, to recognise her individuality and equality as his life partner, to give her kindness and consideration and to support and guide her. His wife undertakes to give him love and respect as well as loyalty and support for his aspirations in life. She agrees to share joys and sorrows and to willingly harmonise her mind and thoughts with his in both affluence and adversity. The formal ceremony is followed by lengthy celebrations and the wedding feast.

Buddha clearly stated the duties of husband and wife to each other but did not specify the need for a marriage ceremony. However, in several parts of the world ceremonies have gradually developed to satisfy the human need for a sense of occasion.

In **Japan**, Shinto priests used to officiate at simple marriage ceremonies but, following a formula initiated by Japanese communities in Hawaii and America, Buddhist ceremonies have become increasingly popular in Japan. They are mainly based on the work of an English priest, the late Ven Ernest Shinkaku Hunt, whose service was adopted in 1924 by the International Buddhist Institute of Hawaii at the Hongwanji in Honolulu, which published a *Vade Mecum* including his marriage service. The ceremony was adopted by Zen and other sects. It includes the typical religious rites of exchanging vows and the signing of a civil register. The ceremony usually takes place during a normal Buddhist gathering, and rings are sometimes exchanged. The marriage certificate is incorporated into a memento booklet along with the text of the service.

For Buddhists in **Thailand** it is a different matter. On the wedding eve, an even number of monks (not less than six) recite Buddhist texts and sprinkle holy water at a chosen place. A sacred cord is bound anticlockwise three times round the pedestal of an image of Buddha and one end of the cord is passed out through a window to encircle the house. After it is bound round their alms-bowls, the other end is held in the monks' hands. In ritual purification, holy water is then sprinkled over the heads of the couple.

On the wedding day, usually in the afternoon, the guests assemble in a waiting-room. The chief guest initiates the ceremony in the next room and then the other guests enter to participate. The couple squat on a low bench, heads bowed and hands held out in an attitude of worship, with the man on the woman's right. Each wears a chaplet of unspun threads. As each guest enters, the master of ceremonies hands them a conch shell containing holy water and, with a blessing, each pours a little water into the couple's hands, letting it flow into a vessel below. Sometimes the conch also contains leaves – either white and green, or red and green. Known respectively as silver leaf and gold leaf, these symbolise wealth. Each guest leaves the room after pouring the water and is given a garland as a memento.

The new **Purple House** in Peking is dedicated to the elimination of China's old feudal wedding customs, which included the bride jumping over a flaming pan to symbolise the severance of her ties with her parents and the letting off of firecrackers to frighten evil spirits. Instead, the Purple House offers (almost as a social service) an all-in Western-style wedding for a price ranging from 900 to 4000 yuan, depending on what the couple want. The average price is about 2500 yuan (less than £300), and that includes lunch for 50 guests (the average monthly wage is only 200 yuan)

and both families share the cost. The venture is a profitable sideline of the Peking Textile Bureau.

The bride wears a white dress and train while the groom wears a black suit and white gloves – both outfits are hired from the Purple House, which also provides make-up artists, for the groom as well as the bride!

Rather than choosing the traditional sedan-chair, the bride might arrive by taxi. Her path is strewn with petals scattered by a girl dressed in pink, to the strains of the Wedding March (on cassette), while video cameras record the event. The guests munch peanuts and drink orange squash while the cheerful master of ceremonies instructs the couple about birth control (the policy in China is one child per couple and the guests no longer put their peanuts in the bridal bed for fertility!).

The best man is likely to be a student on vacation, hired by the Purple House, and the pageboys and bridesmaids are hired from the local kindergarten. They make pocket money by dressing up to look just like the bride and groom in miniature. No longer does the groom hold an arrow against his bride's chest to kill any bad luck, as was traditional, but neither does he kiss the bride.

Guests and their gifts can be received in the Purple House reception room (wedding presents can be bought in the shop on the ground floor) and the Purple House photographer takes the pictures. They can then have a wedding feast or dance, or even a celebratory poetry reading if they prefer. All this is included in the price, along with the bridal suite for the wedding night (a honeymoon elsewhere can be booked through the Purple House). It is what you might call a one-stop wedding!

On the African Loanga coast, a bride and groom must confess their sins to each other during their wedding ceremony. Failure to be honest invites many future illnesses – but no doubt sincerity often leads to sudden changes of heart!

You're sure this is just temporary?

RINGS AND THINGS

The wives of Quichua Indians in Ecuador and northern Peru are given a large, decorative **silver pin** (*topa*) as their marriage token, but in most cultures the custom is to give a **wedding ring**. The wearing of wedding rings probably originated from the Roman custom of giving betrothal rings to confirm secular pledges. A ring symbolises eternity and a binding contract – and possibly also the shackles of a 'captured' bride.

Until the end of the 16th century, it was customary for women in England to wear their wedding rings on the third finger of the *right* hand as a symbol of love and affection (some Catholics still do this). The Ancient Egyptians believed that a delicate nerve ran from this finger to the heart – the Chinese called it a meridian or acupuncture power-line. In 1680, Henry Swinburne named the nerve the *vena amoris* (love vein) in his 'Treaties of Spousals'.

The missals of Hereford, Salisbury and York directed that during the wedding service the ring should be placed first on the thumb, then the forefinger, then the middle and, finally, on the ring finger.

In medieval times (and in the Roman Catholic Church today) the thumb, first and second fingers represented the Trinity; thus the groom said, 'In the name of the Father,' as he touched the thumb, 'In the name of the Son,' for the index finger, 'In the name of the Holy Ghost' for the middle finger, and 'Amen' as he placed the ring on the ring finger.

These days, most people think of a wedding ring as a plain gold band, but different countries around the world have their own popular styles. The Russian wedding ring, for example, has three bands – pink, white and yellow gold – while the Irish claddagh ring is decorated with either a heart or crown and two hands clasped. This style is also favoured in Spain.

In Ireland, the wedding was not recognised as being legal unless the ring was gold. In other countries, however, other items such as brass curtain rings and door keys have served as acceptable substitutes in emergencies.

A ring worn on the forefinger is said to indicate a haughty, bold and overbearing nature while one on the middle finger shows prudence, dignity and discretion – and, on the little finger, masterfulness. The thumb is supposed to be too busy for wedding rings, the forefinger and little finger too unprotected and the middle finger 'too opprobrious for the purpose of honour' – so the third (*pronubus*) finger it must be.

Roman brides wore rings made of iron instead of gold and a favourite design was a pair of hearts linked with a key.

A **gimmal** or **gemel ring** is hinged to form two or three parts (one for the man, one for the woman and perhaps one for the witness) which are united at the marriage ceremony to make a single gold-and-silver wedding ring, sometimes bound with a true lovers' knot. The name has its root in the Latin for 'twin'.

After the Second World War, the European fashion for the bride and groom to exchange wedding rings spread to America, where the bride's ring is usually carried on a white satin cushion by a small boy acting as ring-bearer. In Britain it is the responsibility of the best man.

LEAVING THE CHURCH

After the ceremony comes the celebration. The completion of the formalities is usually signalled by plenty of noise – singing, triumphant music, the pealing of church bells (but if the groom has offended the bellringers, he runs the risk of the luck being bad when they ring the peal backwards), fireworks, foghorns, sirens and gunfire all help to drive away evil and bring good luck as well as to celebrate.

The throwing of **confetti** is an ancient fertility rite, wishing children and prosperity on the couple. The word suggests confectionery (it means 'sweets' in Italian) but originally, and worldwide, **grain** (usually wheat or rice) or **nuts** were thrown; both are 'life-giving' seeds. Nuts also used to be thrown at the couple when they were still at the altar inside the church, and sometimes the vicar was bombarded in error!

At this wedding in July, 1924, fifty British bandsmen played as the couple left the church.

During the Second World War it became popular for guards of honour to stand by the church door as the couple left. Fellow officers of serving men lined up outside the church, making an arch with their dress-swords. The Ministry of Defence issued instructions on the correct way of forming sword-arches and the idea spread. It was common for fellow workers of civilian grooms to make arches appropriate to their trade, and sometimes fellow sportsmen held up golf clubs, tennis racquets or oars (occasionally the last oar was dropped as a 'barring-the-way' ritual and the groom lifted his bride over it).

Today, confetti is usually made of **paper** – which is more a symbol of wanton waste than of fertility – but you can now buy environmentally-friendly, biodegradable confetti based on corn starch (grain) which birds can eat.

Eggs, obvious fertility symbols, are thrown in several European countries and, in Scotland, a cackling **hen** is thrown into the newlyweds' house.

Some weddings are smashing – literally! Among gypsies in Spain, France, Germany and Switzerland it is traditional to break **crockery** after the ceremony. In Peru, the priest at a Chuncho marriage concludes the ceremony by smashing an earthen jar on the ground.

In Ancient Rome, the main wedding procession took place *after* the marriage ceremony, and after nightfall. The bride was escorted from her father's

Fellow diving-club members form a guard of honour after the wedding of a young Belgian couple in Kuurne.

house to the groom's by torchlight, accompanied by flute-players and a large crowd, including local boys chanting rude, jokey verses and petitioning the groom for nuts. When they reached his house, the groom carefully lifted his bride over the threshold (a stumble was a bad omen). Inside the house she was given two symbolic gifts – fire and water, elements so essential to a housewife's duties. On the following day she made her first sacrifices at her husband's altar.

In China, chestnuts are presented to the bride, and in some parts of southern England little baskets of hazelnuts waited for her at the church door. Seeds are typical fertility gifts, especially when enclosed in fruit such as figs and pomegranates, and some North American Indians offer onion seeds.

In Lincolnshire, the congregation used to toss their hassocks at the couple, but the custom was banned after a hassock hit a vicar in 1780.

At Brampton, in Cumbria, formerly in Cumberland, there used to be a lucky 'marriage oak', a relic of the old Celtic tradition of celebrating weddings under an oak tree. Until the tree came down in the mid-19th century, couples continued the ancient custom by hastening to the oak after the church ceremony and dancing round it three times for luck, then carving a little cross on its bark. Many other oaks in villages all over the country once played a similar role.

There is also the delightful custom of planting wedding trees. Typically a tree decorated with ribbons is planted for luck in front of the couple's new home.

PICTURE THIS

The Roman idea of a noisy procession as the couple walked from the ceremony to the wedding celebrations was practised in various ways for many centuries in many countries. Today, the departure from the church or registry office is usually delayed by the demands of the **photographer**. It was in 1854 that a Boston photographer took the earliest known daguerrotype of a bride in her wedding dress (in a studio) and four years later came the first known photographs of bridesmaids – they were attending Queen Victoria's eldest daughter, Princess Vicky, at her wedding to Crown Prince Frederick of Prussia.

By the late 1860s, photographers were increasingly in demand and they progressed to taking outdoor pictures of wedding groups. In 1875, an advertiser in the *Surrey Comet* promised: 'Wedding Parties photographed at any distance' (one wonders at the power of his zoom lens!). At first, the clients were very wealthy and the groups were photographed against a background of stately homes and upper-class gardens, but by Edwardian times *everyone* wanted their wedding photographed.

Reports of society weddings in the press (which have appeared since the 18th century) originally showed sketches of only the heads and shoulders of the couple, dressed in evening or best day-clothes. The report carried full details of the bride's wedding dress and the clothes worn by the bridesmaids and the bride's mother. By the 1890s, however, the papers were publishing photographs of the bride in her wedding dress.

Many couples are whisked to their reception by cars bedecked with white ribbons but many others now choose more interesting forms of transport. When Jonathan Spencer married Clare in her pretty local parish church by the South Downs, they left the church in a pony-drawn trap and, after a garden reception at her parents' home nearby, they were whisked off to their wedding night destination by helicopter, to the complete surprise of the bride.

Mark and Josephine Henshall may have had a conventional wedding at Chiddingfold Parish Church in Surrey, but they made their departure by hot-air balloon! They touched down at a local cricket match to catch the last few overs of the game and then headed for a honeymoon in Florence – but not in the balloon.

Since the 1920s, the fashion has been for the couple to be photographed as they leave the church, and more recently they have even been pictured inside the church. Some vicars also allow video-cameras into the church as the demand for home videos of every stage of the wedding ceremony and celebrations increases.

PARTY TIME

Like the wedding procession, the **wedding feast** is an excuse for the families to show off their wealth. In the West it is the custom for the bride's family to foot the bill for the celebrations and modern fathers can be thankful that the old habit of extending them over several days is no longer expected.

The wedding feast is another rite of passage. By everyone eating and drinking together, the couple

The word bridal comes originally from 'bride ale', a celebration at which ale was the chief liquor. Sometimes the bride herself would brew a good strong ale – and then sell it to her guests.

The Peasant Wedding *by David Teniers.*

are welcomed into their new social group, and in some traditions the marriage is not deemed binding until the bride and groom have shared food and drink. In **Russia**, a bride sprinkles her new husband's food and drink with rosewater to ensure his future faithfulness.

At **Sikh** wedding receptions there are lots of speeches, poem recitals, and singing of songs composed by close relatives and friends of the couple. Then each guest personally congratulates them, putting banknotes in their hands and also (among Sikhs in the West) domestic wedding presents. The feast can be served in the Gurdwara (Sikh temple) but no meat or alcohol is allowed there and richer families tend to go to hotels or restaurants.

At **Celtic** weddings in times gone by, young men known as strawboys gatecrashed the party disguised in straw suits and masks. Their leader,

In 1988, Saul Steinberg threw a wedding party for his daughter at the Metropolitan Museum of Art in New York – it cost about $3 million.

In Flint, Michigan, in 1990, 15 important drug pushers from Corunna were among the guests at a wedding. The bride, Debra Williams, lifted her skirts to remove her garter but instead she pulled out a handgun – she was an undercover police officer. Most of the guests also pulled out guns – they, too, were police. Their cue for action was when the band played the song *I Fought The Law*.

A wedding breakfast, English style, as caricatured in 1849. The bride looks remarkably like Queen Victoria!

often a previously rejected suitor, claimed the right to dance with the bride.

In some cultures it is the custom to dance – and dance and dance – until the guests drop. In **Hungary**, guests used to take part in all-night gymnastics – after a ten-course dinner! In **Salamanca**, in Spain, anyone who danced with the bride left a coin under a pie-crust at her table, and in **Poland** dancers pinned banknotes to the bride's dress while the groom collected coins in a large apron pocket as he danced.

In the 19th century, the **bidden wedding** sometimes took place instead of a wedding-day feast, either on the day or at a later date in the new marital home. It was customary for the guests to bring money and presents to give the couple a good start in their married life, and sometimes an ox-drawn, gaily decorated wagon (known as a 'bridewain') travelled around the neighbourhood collecting presents for the newlyweds. In Wales and Holland, particularly persuasive talkers drummed up guests, 'bidding' as many people as possible to come to the party and bring their gifts.

Beware of strange old men at your wedding! Like the Ancient Mariner, one of the most famous and persistent uninvited wedding guests of all – you know the type:

'It is an ancient Mariner,
 And he stoppeth one of three.
"By thy long grey beard and glittering
  eye,
 Now wherefore stopp'st thou me?" . . .
He holds him with his skinny hand . . .
He holds him with his glittering eye –
 The Wedding-Guest stood still,
And listens like a three years' child:
 The Mariner hath his will.
The Wedding-Guest sat on a stone:
 He cannot choose but hear;
And thus spake on that ancient man . . .'

Samuel Taylor Coleridge *The Ancient Mariner*

In April, 1990, Mr John 'Dapper Don' Gotti staged a lavish celebration for the marriage of his son, John Gotti Jnr, to Miss Kim Albanese, daughter of a carpet contractor. The venue was the luxurious Helmsley Palace Hotel in New York's Madison Avenue. The hotel's owner, Mrs Leona Helmsley, was about to start a four-year prison sentence for tax fraud, and 'Dapper Don' was the reigning Mafia godfather of what the police referred to as the 'Gambino crime family'. Large numbers of invited guests arrived in huge black Cadillacs, including many of the most important old families. They danced the tarantella and feasted on veal, lobster and fettucine alfredo, while admiring the low-cut off-the-shoulder dresses of the bride and bridesmaids. Taking every precaution, the Don had booked every ballroom and reception area in the hotel and his burly guards kept out a host of eager gatecrashers, including the media and the FBI. They had already fooled these unwanted guests over the location of the church ceremony by setting off on tortuous drives through the suburbs, followed by panting newshounds and the police, and duping television crews into setting up their cameras outside several local churches where other weddings were taking place. The whole affair was reminiscent of Marlon Brando's famous film, *The Godfather*, except that no deaths were reported.

In the northern village of Rajpura, in Uttar Pradesh, a peasant wedding feast led to the deaths of more than 200 guests. At the time, most of the local doctors were in jail for staging an illegal strike, but they were rapidly released to deal with the catastrophe, which was found to be due to the recent heavy use of pesticides on the local crops, which had provided flour for the feast's delicacies.

The better the promised entertainment on offer, the more generous the gifts would be. There was however, a catch to these bidden gifts – later on, the couple might have to give similar presents to a couple of the original giver's choice.

In **Britain** in 1989, more than 600 guests at ten different wedding receptions suffered from salmonella poisoning. The main culprits were beef and cold turkey, although there were many more unreported cases which had resulted from prawns, chicken, roast pork, chocolate mousse, vegetarian quiches and egg dishes. After one wedding reception at the famous Savoy hotel in London, the bride's Florida honeymoon was ruined – she was ill for five days after eating salmon in a champagne sauce. At the Blenheim Palace wedding of the Marquess of Blandford a year later, the 600 guests were more carefully served – the caterers used only pasteurised eggs in their canapes. Environmental health consultant, Roger North, advised: 'Brides and grooms intent on enjoying their honeymoons would perhaps be best advised to take a leaf out of the airline pilot's book and eat meals that are different to those of their guests – steak and chips, eaten immediately after they are cooked, would be a safe bet. But perhaps the real answer is to live in sin!'

When Menachem Teitelbaum married Brucha Meisels in December, 1984, 150 buses transported more than 20 000 guests to the pre-wedding reception at Nassau Coliseum, home of the New York Islanders ice hockey team, but only 8000 went to the sit-down dinner afterwards.

Mohammed, son of Sheikh Rashid Bin Saeed Al Maktoum, married Princess Salama in Dubai in May, 1981. The whole affair lasted seven days and cost about £22 million.

People in Britain used to save the bones from the wedding feast and carve them into lace-bobbins which they inscribed to make lucky love tokens.

LET THEM EAT CAKE

The **wedding cake** is often the centre of the wedding feast today; it has an ancient history as a symbol of good luck and fertility – hence all the fruit in it. In several countries, it is traditional to have two cakes – a rich fruity one for the groom and a lighter one for the bride. As a compromise, a fruit cake

'Dreaming bread' was the piece of cake an unmarried girl kept under her pillow to make her dream of her future husband. Before putting it there she passed it through a wedding ring three times. It was believed that a bride should keep a piece of her wedding cake to ensure her husband's fidelity – at least until the first child had been born, after which the piece of cake was eaten at the child's christening feast.

can be covered with white icing to represent the bride's part and in America the cake is often a mixture of colours, in different tiers, but it is always white-iced, and sometimes the cake is ring-shaped.

In Bermuda, the groom's wedding cake is wreathed in ivy to symbolise affection. The bride's cake is topped with a tree seedling, which is ceremoniously planted during the evening wedding reception and carefully tended by the couple for many years as a symbol of their flourishing marriage. Some British couples plant trees on their wedding anniversary as a long-lasting tribute of their love for each other.

As with almost every other wedding item, there are plenty of superstitions surrounding the cake. For example, every guest must eat at least a crumb of the cake. To refuse a piece is said to bring bad luck on the couple as well as on the guilty guest. The gesture of sending pieces of the cake to those who could not attend the wedding is fairly recent, but it enables them to share in the good luck it is thought to bring.

It is considered unlucky for the bride to bake her own cake, but at the feast she should cut the first slice (with her husband placing a helping hand on hers) to ensure that the marriage produces children. Some say the couple should also share the last slice. In America, the couple feed the first slice to each other.

According to the diaries of John Evelyn (1620–1706) it was the custom for the bride and groom to 'kiss over the bride-cakes' at the table towards the end of the feast. The bride-cakes were buns or biscuits laid on top of each other 'in the manner of shew-bread' (12 Jewish loaves) pictured in old bibles.

Futuristic wedding cake: this photo (taken in 1954) shows confectioner, Raymond Wall, with the cake he designed for AD 2000. It appeared on the 'Britain Can Bake It' stand at the International Exhibition of Gastronomy and Tourism in Munich.

In Scotland, Yorkshire and Lincolnshire there used to be a custom of throwing a plateful of cake (or shortbread in Scotland) over the bride's head as she returned from church or came into her new home, with the intention of the plate smashing to smithereens (not actually *on* her head – the plate landed beyond her!). Some said that the more fragments there were, the happier the marriage would be, while others thought that the number of fragments represented the number of children that would be born in the marriage.

In the 16th and 17th centuries, the cake was made of wheat or barley and it was sometimes divided into fingers, which were passed through the wedding ring (they were small fingers!) to bring good luck and to hasten the marital prospects of the single.

The marzipan (almond paste) on a cake is doubly symbolic – it promises fertility because it is made from nuts, and it blends the bitterness and sweetness of marriage.

The favourite lovebird of Aphrodite (the Greek goddess of beauty) was the dove, which is now a popular wedding cake decoration. The bird was considered sacred in many ancient religions and was regarded as a symbol of purity, peace and tender love. Other favourite cake decorations include wedding bells, lucky horseshoes and cupids.

Sugared almonds are traditional wedding sweets or bride-cakes, especially in France and Italy, but in the Netherlands the bitter-sweet aspects of marriage were symbolised by salted cream sprinkled with sugar.

OVER THE THRESHOLD

Thresholds are dangerous places for one whose life is radically changing. All over the world there are threshold rituals, which are performed either to frighten off those wretched evil spirits or to invite fertility and prosperity. Usually these rituals involve symbolic items such as seed, grain, fruit, foliage, flowers, honey, yeast and dairy produce.

Tradition dictates that a new wife must enter her new home by the main door, and to avoid bad luck she must put her right foot across its threshold first. Better still, her husband should carry her safely over it. If the sun happens to be shining at this time it is an extremely good omen.

In places as far apart as Yorkshire and Italy, **thresholds** and **hot water** have important parts to play in the rituals. As the bride leaves her family home for the last time, she paddles her shoes in hot water, which has been poured on the threshold, to encourage another wedding among the assembly (it is supposed to be arranged before the water dries).

Other threshold rituals can be smelly affairs. In the hill villages of western Nepal, as well as in India, cows are sacred and beloved animals and a new bride steps over or through a pile of cowdung so that she will be like the cow – serene and at peace with the world.

BEDDING THE BRIDE

Bedding the bride (ie literally putting her to bed) used to be an acceptable, public and thoroughly gleeful part of the wedding celebrations. Either the family or the bridesmaids and groom's men joined in, and sometimes most of the village as well, with much horseplay. Sometimes the priest introduced a solemn interlude by giving the couple the **benediction posset**, a sanctified sweetened wine. The rest of the guests were plied with sack-posset (an eggnog of milk, eggs, sugar, sack and nutmeg) while the couple tried to steal away from the party unnoticed.

In the bridal chamber, the groom would be undressed by his men while the bridesmaids undressed the bride. The girl who drew out the first **pin** from the bride's clothes would be the first in the group to marry but all the pins had to be removed, and then thrown away, to protect the bride from bad luck. If the bridesmaid kept a pin it was said that she would not marry for a long time.

Once the couple had been formally bedded by the company, the bridesmaids sat on one side of the bed and the groom's men on the other (or all sat at the foot of the bed) with their backs to the newlyweds. The girls took the groom's **stockings** and the men the bride's, then they simultaneously tossed them over their shoulders at the couple. If

Bedding the bride: Jan Steen's Peasants' Wedding *(1670) shows the bride being encouraged towards the bridal chamber, with much ribaldry.*

one of the bride's stockings hit the groom, or the groom's hit the bride, the person who had thrown it would marry soon after.

The marital bed was not a quiet place that night. In Sweden, a **baby** might have been laid to sleep with the couple to bring them fertility. In Ireland, for the same reason, a **laying hen** was tied to the bedpost, though elsewhere pictures of fruit or flowers, or items of children's furniture, did the trick. More sedately, brides in Germany, Algeria and elsewhere would sew certain symbols into the **quilt** or **mattress**, to ensure fidelity as well as fertility.

The guests were often determined that the newlyweds should have no chance of sleep on their wedding night – they would keep up a great din outside the bridal chamber all night long in the form of '**rough music**'. The Spanish would sing rude songs until the groom let them know that all

had gone well – news which was greeted with much cheering and whistling.

The custom of disappearing to a secret honeymoon destination has put paid to most of these old customs. Only the tin cans clattering behind the departing car are a reminder of how it used to be.

On the island of Lamu, which is just off the Kenyan coast, marital beds are smothered with jasmine flowers for the wedding night. And in both China and Morocco, a bride yields to her husband in candlelight so that she is seen in a soft glow. Some say that the consummation of a marriage is most fulfilling and most fertile if the waxing moon is almost full on the night.

Twin-heart swimming pool at Honeymoon Haven in the Pocono Mountains, Pennsylvania (1968). This was just one of six local resorts catering exclusively for newly-weds.

PETTICOATS AND TROUSERS

With the wedding over, the battle of the sexes begins in earnest. There are countless superstitions and rituals to determine which partner will be dominant in the marriage. Here are a few of them:

The bride gets the upper hand if she puts her **right foot** ahead of the groom's at the altar rail, but the bride who steps out of the church **left foot** first will be dominated. And whoever is first to make a **purchase** after the ceremony will hold the purse-strings – so, girls, have a bridesmaid stationed at the church door and buy a token from her on the way out!

Parsley grows best where 'the mistress is master' as long as she sows the seed herself, and the same is true of **rosemary** bushes and **sage**. So, if you see a flourishing sage bush in a garden, you can be sure that the wife wears the trousers.

Whichever partner manages to tread on the other's **foot** first in the marital home will rule the household – a ritual which can cause chaos at the threshold! Worse still, in the Moroccan marital bedroom there is a **slipper** fight – when the hus-

An old woman of the Afikpo Ibo tribe in south-east Nigeria declared proudly: 'Nowadays women do not care if the husband doesn't give them any food, for they can go to the farm and get cassava (the staple crop). The year after she does this, she can have her own crop for cassava meal, which she can sell and have her own money. Then she can say: "What is man? I have my own money! I need no man!"'

Millicent Barclay had the last laugh.
The daughter of Colonel William Barclay, she was born in July, 1872, after his death. Thus she immediately became eligible for a Madras Military Fund pension, to be paid to her until she married – but she never did. Instead she drew her pension for 97 years and 3 months, dying a spinster in October, 1969.

band first enters his new wife's room he has his right slipper at the ready and she is similarly armed ready to strike the first blow and assert her dominance.

UNCONVENTIONAL WEDDINGS
Quick weddings, known as **liberty weddings**, used to be carried out illicitly by clergy of Trinity Minorities and St James's, Duke's Place, who claimed immunity from the Bishop of London's jurisdiction.

Similarly, **Fleet marriages** were clandestine weddings, often involving minors, without any reading of banns or licences. They were performed by the clergy of the chapel of The Fleet, a famous London debtors' prison in Farringdon Street which was demolished in 1845 (the Memorial Hall was built on its site). The Fleet's clergymen needed money and would perform marriage ceremonies at night in private houses and pubs nearby, and no questions were asked. There were even men outside drumming up business for them, offering instant marriages, much like the Soho doormen offer other 'delights' to tourists today. Some of the customers were unwilling ones – perhaps the drunken victims of frustrated or indebted women seeking marriages of convenience. Many a sailor woke up with a hangover and a wife he had never seen before. In the four months to February, 1705, nearly 3000 such marriages were registered, including 30 couples married in a single day by one clergyman, and at least 80 Fleet parsons' names were recorded.

They had their rivals at Curzon Street, also in London, where notorious and irregular **Mayfair**

The Sailor's Fleet Wedding Entertainment (1747). *A classic case of the drunken sailor trapped into instant marriage with a total stranger. Note the allegorical cat and dog representing marital strife.*

Le Mariage Clandestin – *a French version of the Fleet weddings.*

marriages were performed by the Rev Alexander Keith. One of the most famous was the wedding of the sixth Duke of Hamilton to the younger of the two beautiful Miss Gunnings, in 1752. The ceremony took place at 12.30 am and a bed-curtain ring was the wedding ring. Several lords, viscounts and other nobles went through curtain-ring wedding ceremonies in Keith's Mayfair chapel.

Flagg Marriages were the American equivalent of the Fleet and Mayfair marriages, and were carried out by Parson Flagg of Chester, Vermont, who always had a large stock of marriage certificates to hand.

The **1753 Marriage Act** brought these anomalies to an end under English law by preventing the marriage of minors without parental consent and by insisting on the calling of banns and the need to be married in a church or chapel. The penalty for offenders was often transportation. But lovers were not easily thwarted and the English merely headed over the border to Scotland, where they could legally marry as minors, or without a licence or banns, or even a priest. They simply declared their willingness to marry before

witnesses. The most popular witnesses were blacksmiths but there were also landlords, toll-keepers, fishermen, shoemakers – anyone who was willing to help, for a small fee or a drink.

Gretna Green was the first place across the border for eloping English couples – it is only

The 'Bride of the Sea' is Venice and ever since a Venetian naval victory in the 10th century it has been the custom for the Doge (Mayor) of Venice to perform the Wedding of the Sea ceremony in commemoration of the victory. In 1177, Pope Alexander III gave the Doge his gold ring as a token of gratitude for saving the Papacy by the Venetian fleet's victory over Frederick Barbarossa. Thereafter, the Doge has blessed a gold ring and thrown it into the sea during the Ascension Day ceremony, declaring, 'We wed thee, O sea, in token of perpetual domination.'

Gretna Green, just over the border into Scotland, where English couples could instantly and legally marry. The blacksmith was a popular witness in place of a priest.

seven or eight miles north-west of Carlisle, but several other Borders settlements were involved. One such was **Coldstream**, where the last recognised semi-professional witness was a shoe-maker, Willie Dickson, who had taken over the job from a mole-catcher. The Coldstream ceremonies were at the Bridge End Inn.

The **1856 Marriage Act** made it necessary for at least one of the pair to reside in Scotland for at least 21 days before the crossborder marriage, which took some of the romantic impulsiveness out of it all. Minors can still marry in Scotland without parental consent, but marriage by declara-tion ceased to be legal from July, 1940.

Smock weddings are connected with debt. In England, it was long believed that a woman's hus-band could not be held responsible for debts she had incurred before their marriage, if she came to her wedding dressed only in a smock or shift (or even a sheet) and with bare feet – or, if she was brave, walked from her home to her groom's wear-ing nothing at all. She had effectively shed her debts with her clothes (the wearing of the smock was only a concession to decency) and, by going naked and without possessions to her own wed-ding, she showed publicly that she brought noth-ing to the marriage. Therefore no claim could be made on the groom for her debts.

In 1835, a parish church in **Manchester** reduced its fees for Easter weddings and found itself with a queue of 197 couples. The marriage was started en masse, at 10 am.

Later in the 19th century, there was a similar mass wedding on a popular date (probably Easter) at **Broussa** in Armenia. The place was packed with relatives and friends, and all the brides were dressed identically and wore heavy crimson veils. At least two couples were mismatched – a pretty peasant girl married a wealthy man by mistake, and

In 1974, there was a national rail strike in India which stranded an estimated 200 000 Hindu couples who were due to marry. Because the exact timing of a Hindu marriage is carefully chosen as propitious, many had to delay their weddings until the next most favourable moment. One groom in Bombay gathered his party into a fleet of taxis and drove at full pelt across 1500 miles (2414km) to his bride in Calcutta. It took them three days to get there but they arrived two hours too late and everything had to be deferred to the following year.

a plain but rich girl married a blacksmith. Happily, they stayed that way.

In the middle of the 19th century, four couples held a joint wedding ceremony in the **Yorkshire Dales**. Seven men on horseback carried the four brides and three attendants behind them in the saddle. Everyone else came on horseback too, including a group of young men firing off their guns as the procession arrived at the church gate.

A real **shotgun wedding** is one entered into under duress – usually ordered by the irate father of a pregnant girl.

At Seoul in South Korea, in October, 1982, the Rev **Sun Myung Moon**, of the Holy Spirit Association for the Unification of World Christianity, officiated at the simultaneous marriages of 5837 couples from 83 different countries. In July of the same year he had married 2075 couples at Madison Square Garden in New York. Not content with small numbers, on 30th October, 1988, he officiated at the wedding of 6516 couples at a factory near Seoul.

In 1967, there was a municipally sponsored 'wed-in' at Prospect Park, Brooklyn, New York, with everything paid for by local businesses. Fifty couples were invited to participate but unfortunately only nine took up the offer.

The town of Rheden, in the Netherlands, agreed in October, 1990, to 'spearhead the right to legalise homosexual marriage' when it allowed a marriage ceremony between two men, Gerard Kuipers and Frank Stello, who had been refused permission to marry each other in their home town of Vlaardingen. Perhaps the transsexual model, Caroline Cossey (see p. 34), should try going Dutch.

Here come the brides – all identically dressed. One of Rev Sun Myung Moon's mass-marriage ceremonies, on 8th February, 1975 – he officiated at the simultaneous weddings of 1800 couples from 19 countries, in a Seoul gymnasium.

A MATTER OF CONVENIENCE

There is a time-honoured practice of marriage between partners who have no intention of living together. Usually one partner seeks marriage in order to meet, for example, immigration requirements, and the contract is a mere formality, often in exchange for money. In such cases the marriage certificate is obtained and the couple probably never see each other again after the wedding ceremony.

One British woman is known to have 'married' at least 30 men from West Africa. The case came to light when registrars in several different towns noticed the same bride and witnesses at different weddings, sometimes even in the same week!

It is thought that in 1988 at least 5000 West Africans went through such bogus marriages in Britain, often as a form of insurance against deportation. It was estimated that at least half of West African applications to settle or remain in Britain were based on bogus marriages.

In London in 1990, The Times reported that there were seven ethnic-minority welfare agencies and half a dozen immigration advisers (including lawyers and a Justice of the Peace) helping to organise bogus marriages for immigrants so that they could obtain residence rights. The hopefuls paid up to £2000 to marry a British citizen, who was usually already married, or perhaps a prostitute or an unemployed man, or even, as in one case, a prison officer.

Sometimes immigrants 'marry' by obtaining a copy of a British citizen's birth certificate at random and, for all you know, your own name might have been used as that of a spouse in a bogus wedding ceremony and you could find yourself 'married' to a total stranger! A certain lady was amazed to be told by immigration officials that she had married Mr Frimpong, a student from West Africa whom she had never met. A man working for British Nuclear Fuels was told that he had married a West African woman he'd never heard of – he had never even been to London, where his 'wife' claimed to live with him!

4
Now That We're Married

... I reckon if I play my cards right I would be an alimony millionairess by ex-husband number three!

SHARING

Polygamy is the custom of allowing marriage to more than one person at a time. **Polygyny** is having several wives at a time, which is much more common than **polyandry**, which is having several husbands at a time. **Monogamy** imposes a limit of one husband or wife at a time (**monogyny** for one wife, **monandry** for one husband). **Bigamy** is the custom (or crime, in many countries) of having two wives or husbands at the same time.

Many cultures regard a man's need for numerous children (especially sons) to be paramount and therefore accept and encourage polygyny.

This is especially true in parts of Africa where women abstain from sex after giving birth, often until the child is weaned. In 1959, about 35% of all African husbands were polygynous, and they averaged about 2.5 wives each. The highest rate of polygyny at the time was along the Guinea coast, where 43% of all married men had more than one wife.

For a **Ngombe** man living near the Congo river, it was of supreme importance that his name lived on in the memories of future generations and therefore he needed lots of wives so that he could

Cheerful polygamy: Swedish citizen Matti Soukka married two wives in Zambia in accordance with local customs, but the Swedish authorities were so shocked when he came home that they only gave him a temporary tourist's visa. Later they relented and by October, 1984, Matti and his two wives and five children were allowed to settle in Sweden as one big happy family.

The Yatenga Mossi of Upper Volta had a well-organised society 50 years ago with a king, four provincial grand ministers, chiefs for each canton within each province, and a chief for each village within each canton. The village was composed of 'quarters', which were dwellings for extended families. The oldest male was head of household and provided separate houses for his wives, for his younger brothers and their wives, and for his sons, nephews, cousins and their wives and children. Each adult had a separate house and garden within the quarter. Any man could have several wives and each was given a house adjoining the husband's. The daughters left the quarter on marriage and were expected to carry the extended family's good name to their husbands' households.

It was rumoured that King George III's brother, the Duke of Cumberland, had married a clergyman's daughter, Olive Wilmot, and less than a year later he bigamously married widow Anne Horton, but no one really knew the truth of the matter. The King's other brother, the Duke of Gloucester, secretly married the Dowager Countess Waldegrave, the illegitimate daughter of Prime Minister Walpole's son; and the King's sister, Caroline Matilda, who was married to Christian VII of Denmark, had an outrageous affair with her husband's adviser. She was promptly banished from Denmark and her lover was put to death. Despairing of his own family, George III introduced the Royal Marriage Act in 1772, decreeing that royals must gain their sovereign's permission to marry.

Brigham Young (1801–1877) was born at Whitingham, Vermont, and became a carpenter, painter and glazier in Mendon, New York. He was converted to Mormonism in 1832 and eventually led a huge group of displaced Mormons to Utah to found Salt Lake City. The Mormons had been founded by Vermont-born Joseph Smith (1805–1844) and their doctrines included polygamy, but Utah was only admitted as a State on condition that polygamy was prohibited. The sect did not relent until 1890, long after Young's death. He was a farsighted administrator of his flourishing city, and when he died he left $2 500 000 to his 17 wives and 56 children.

father lots of children. Each wife occupied a separate room in his household, or, for preference, he built a new house for each new wife and helped her make a garden.

In the 1480s, the **Oba of Benin**, in West Africa, promised to encourage all his subjects to become Catholics in return for a Portuguese wife. Both sides stuck to the terms of the bargain. In 1897, the then Oba had 80 wives and plenty of concubines as well but they all had to be sent back to their families when he was exiled to Calabar by the English after a massacre (which had arisen from an unfortunate misunderstanding). He begged to be allowed to take his two favourite wives with him and this was granted.

In the Cameroons, a prince might have six wives but most men have no more than three, though in the 1920s one man claimed that he had 99 wives.

In parts of **Brazil**, **Tibet** and **New Guinea**, a man shares his wife with his father. In **Zaïre** and **Bolivia**, a woman shares her husband with her mother. Among several **Asian** mountain tribes, women share their husbands, while in certain **West African** tribes, wives are shared.

Women who form part of a rich man's **harem** are not resentful of their lot. Indeed, it gives them a feeling of sisterhood and also, for some, relieves individual women of the perpetual 'burden' of a man's sexual appetite!

Mozart's well-loved opera, *The Marriage of Figaro*, has been translated into Arabic by Egyptian anaesthetist, Aly Sadek, a passionate opera buff who wants to bring opera to the masses. His version (along with one of *Cosi Fan Tutte*) has been recorded by Arabic singers supported by the Polish National Orchestra, and it is hoped that there will be a performance at the recently restored Cairo Opera House. *The Times*, tongue in cheek, suggested that *Il Seraglio* (meaning harem) seemed a more apposite choice for a Muslim audience and that the Mozart translation might become *The Marriages of Figaro*.

King Solomon, who was famous for his wisdom, apparently had 700 wives and countless mistresses. Clearly he had a way with women! The *Song of Solomon* in the Old Testament is rich with phrases of love and flattery of women – including verses such as 'Thy hair is as a flock of goats', and 'Thy teeth are like a flock of sheep that are even shorn'(!) – but there is no proof that the King had any hand in composing the songs.

THE MORE THE MERRIER

Don Juan Tenorio was the son of an aristocratic 14th-century family in Seville. It is said that he seduced the daughter of the commandant of Ulloa and then killed him. He came to represent the arch seducer and libertine, something of a suave 'Hooray Henry' and the anti-hero of many novels and plays. As well as being a model for Lord Byron in both real life and in his works, Don Juan was the basis of Mozart's *Don Giovanni* (written in 1787) in which his valet claims that his dissolute master had 700 mistresses in Italy, 800 in Germany, 91 in Turkey and France, and 1003 in Spain. Much of the lothario's energy and wits were devoted to keeping his women apart and unaware of each

The last Sharifian Emperor of Morocco, Moulay Ismael the Bloodthirsty, who lived from 1672 to 1727, had fathered 525 sons and 342 daughters by 1703, and his 700th son was born in 1721.

Bluebeard was the unpleasant tyrant in Perrault's *Contes de Temps* (1697) who had a habit of murdering his wives and storing all their bodies in a locked room in his castle.

other's existence – no doubt a modern Don Juan could find a use for the electronic pass systems which today keep unwanted intruders out of security zones.

The Chinese Emperor, **Yang-Ti**, liked to have about 4000 women at his beck and call, including 3000 palace 'maidens' as well as his various queens and consorts. **King Mongut** of Siam, who died in 1868, was said to have 9000 wives and concubines – perhaps Yul Brynner should have starred in *The King and We!*

Giovanni Vigliotto, also known as Fred Jipp, Nikolai Peruskov and about 50 other aliases, was sentenced in Phoenix, Arizona, to 28 years' imprisonment for fraud. He was also fined $336 000 and given six years for bigamy. Between 1949 and 1981 he had a total of 104 bigamous marriages, four of them on board one ship in 1968!

In 1922, in Sheffield, 24-year-old **Theresa Vaughan** apparently confessed during a trial that she had had 61 bigamous marriages within five years, but local police records could not confirm her case.

THE ODD COUPLE

Sir Robert Mayer, Companion of Honour, was 101 years old when he married Jacqueline Noble in London, in November, 1980. She was half his age.

Harry Stevens was 103 when he married his 84-year-old cousin Thelma Lucas in December, 1984.

Mrs Winifred Clark was a day short of her 100th birthday when she married Albert Smith (then aged 80) in Yorkshire in November, 1971.

Wrestler Martin Ruane (alias Luke McMasters or Giant Haystacks) was born at Camberwell in 1946 and has weighed up to 50 stone (317.5kg). His bride, Rita, weighed 7 st 7lb (47.6kg) at their wedding.

Jon Brower Minnoch weighed 92 st 12lb (589kg) when he married Jeanette, who weighed 7 st 12lb (49.9kg) in March, 1978.

Nigel Wilks of Kingston-on-Hull and Beverly Russell were both born in 1963; they married in June, 1984. He is 6ft 7in (2m) tall and she, who suffers from the skeletal disorder achondroplasia, is only 3ft 11in (1.2m). Their son Daniel was delivered by Caesarean section and weighed 9lb 5oz (4.2kg) at his birth in March, 1986.

Richard Gibson, a well-regarded portrait painter born in 1615, and his wife Anne (née Shepherd) were both 3ft 10in (1.1m) tall.

Charles S Stratton, born at Bridgeport, Connecticut, in 1838, was known as General Tom Thumb. When he married Lavinia Warren in 1863, he was 2ft 10in (86cm) tall and she 2 inches shorter. In 1884, the widowed Lavinia married Count Primo Magri, who was also 2ft 8in (81cm) tall.

Captain Martin van Buren Bates of Whitesbury, Kentucky, married Anna Hanen Swan of Nova Scotia at St Martin-in-the-Fields, London, on 17th June, 1871. Both claimed to be half an inch short of 8ft (2.4m) tall but, as giants often do, they had exaggerated. In fact she was 7ft 5½in (2.3m) and he was 7ft 2½in (2.2m). However, they remain the tallest married couple on record.

The first woman in space, Valentina V Tereshkova (born in 1937), married another space traveller, Andreyan Grigoryevich Nikolayev, in November, 1963, less than 5 months after her flight of 48 orbits of the earth (1 225 000 miles). Her husband had completed 64 orbits (1 640 000 miles) in August, 1962.

Right: Grandson and grandmother or husband and wife? Ruth and Kevin Kimber were married in August, 1990, when she was 93 and he was 28, but the age gap doesn't seem to matter. True love knows no bounds . . .

Below: A gigantic affair: the wedding of Captain Martin van Buren Bates and Anna Hanen Swan in London in 1871, the tallest married couple of record (see p. 118).

HEARTFELT WORDS

" ————————————

It is a truth universally acknowledged, that a single man in possession of a good fortune, must be in want of a wife.

Jane Austen *Pride and Prejudice*

————————————"

" ————————————

One was never married, and that's his hell; another is, and that's his plague.

Robert Burton *Democritus to the Reader*

————————————"

" ————————————

Wedlock, indeed, hath oft compared been
To public feasts where meet a public rout,
Where they that are without would fain go in
And they that are within would fain go out.

Sir John Davies *A Contention Betwixt a Wife, a Widow, and a Maid for Precedence*

————————————"

" ————————————

Every woman should marry – and no man.

Benjamin Disraeli *Lothair*

————————————"

" ————————————

It is a woman's business to get married as soon as possible, and a man's to keep unmarried as long as he can.

George Bernard Shaw *Man and Superman*

————————————"

" ————————————

In her first passion, woman loves her lover. In all the others, all she loves is love.

Lord Byron *Don Juan*

————————————"

" ————————————

A woman, let her be as good as she may, has got to put up with the life her husband makes for her.

George Eliot *Middlemarch*

————————————"

" ————————————

Courtship to marriage, as a very witty prologue to a very dull Play.

William Congreve *The Old Bachelor*

————————————"

" ————————————

Man's love is of man's life a thing apart,
'Tis woman's whole existence.

Lord Byron *Don Juan*

————————————"

" ————————————

I never mused a dear Gazelle, to glad me with its soft black eye, but when it came to know me well, and love me, it was sure to marry a market-gardener.

Charles Dickens *The Old Curiosity Shop*

————————————"

" ————————————

Marriage is the proper Remedy. It is the most natural State of Man, and therefore the State in which you will find solid happiness.

Benjamin Franklin

————————————"

" ————————————

Do you think your mother and I should have liv'd comfortably so long together, if ever we had been married?

John Gay *The Beggar's Opera*

————————————"

"

You, that are going to be married, think things can never be done too fast; but we, that are old, and know what we are about, must elope methodically, madam.

Oliver Goldsmith *The Good-Natured Man*

"

"

Marriage the happiest bond of love might be,
If hands were only joined when hearts agree.

George Granville, Baron Lansdowne *The British Enchanters*

"

"

I drew my bride, beneath the moon,
Across my threshold; happy hour!

Coventry Patmore *The Angel in the House*

"

"

Men are April when they woo,
December when they wed; maids are May when they are maids, but the sky changes when they are wives.

Shakespeare *As You Like It*

"

"

Those who talk most about the blessings of marriage and the constancy of its vows are the very people who declare that if the chain were broken and the prisoners left free to choose, the whole social fabric would fly asunder. You cannot have the argument both ways. If the prisoner is happy, why lock him in? If he is not, why pretend he is?

George Bernard Shaw *Major Barbara*

"

"

It is so far from being natural for a man and woman to live in a state of marriage that we find all the motives which they have for remaining in that connection, and the restraints which civilized society imposes to prevent separation, are hardly sufficient to keep them together.

Samuel Johnson

"

"

Marriage is popular because it combines the maximum of temptation with the maximum of opportunity.

George Bernard Shaw *Man and Superman*

"

"

In marriage, a man becomes slack and selfish, and undergoes a fatty degeneration of his mortal being.

Robert Louis Stevenson *Virginibus Puerisque*

"

"

What woman, however old, has not the bridal-favours and raiment stowed away, and packed in lavender, in the inmost cupboards of her heart?

William Makepeace Thackeray *Lovel the Widower*

"

"

Marriage is the result of the longing for the deep, deep peace of the double bed after the hurly-burly of the chaise-longue.

Ascribed to the actress, Mrs Patrick Campbell

"

"
All comedies are ended by a marriage.

Lord Byron *Don Juan*
"

"
Marriage is like life in this – that it is a field of battle, and not a bed of roses.

Robert Louis Stevenson *Virginibus Puerisque*
"

"
The happy married man dies in good stile at home, surrounded by his weeping wife and children. The old batchelor don't die at all – he sort of rots away, like a polly-wog's tail.

Charles Farrar Browne *Artemus Ward His Book*
"

"
Wives are young men's mistresses, companions for middle age, and old men's nurses.

Francis Bacon *Of Marriage and Single Life*
"

"
It was very good of God to let Carlyle and Mrs Carlyle marry one another and so make only two people miserable.

Samuel Butler, in a letter
"

"
My mistress' eyes are nothing like the sun;
Coral is far more red than her lips' red;
If snow be white, why then her breasts are dun;
If hairs be wires, black wires grow on her head.

William Shakespeare *Sonnets*
"

"
'Tis melancholy, and a fearful sign
Of human frailty, folly, also crime,
That love and marriage rarely can combine,
Although they both are born in the same clime;
Marriage from love, like vinegar from wine –
A sad, sour, sober beverage – by time
Is sharpen'd from its high celestial flavour,
Down to a very homely household savour.

Lord Byron *Don Juan*
"

"
Married women are kept women, and they are beginning to find it out.

Logan Pearsall Smith *Other People*
"

"
Marriage is the waste-paper basket of the emotions.

Attributed to Sidney Webb
"

"
As the husband is, the wife is: thou art mated with a clown,
And the grossness of his nature will have weight to drag thee down.
He will hold thee, when his passion shall have spent its novel force,
Something better than his god, a little dearer than his horse.

Alfred, Lord Tennyson *Locksley Hall*
"

"
There is no fury like an ex-wife searching for a new lover.

Cyril Connolly *The Unquiet Grave*
"

"

Let us be very strange and well-bred:
Let us be as strange as if we have been
married a great while, and as well-bred
as if we were not married at all.

William Congreve *The Way of the World*

"

"

Lord Illingworth: 'The Book of Life
begins with a man and a woman in a
garden.' Mrs Allonby: 'It ends with
Revelations.'

Oscar Wilde *A Woman of No Importance*

"

"

The comfortable estate of widowhood,
is the only hope that keeps up a wife's
spirits.

John Gay *The Beggar's Opera*

"

"

If I continue to endure you a little
longer, I may by degrees dwindle into a
wife.

William Congreve *The Way of the World*

"

"

Marriage has many pains, but celibacy
has no pleasures.

Samuel Johnson *Rasselas*

"

"

Thy husband is thy lord, thy life, thy
keeper,
Thy head, thy sovereign; one that cares
for thee,
And for thy maintenance commits his
body
To painful labour both by sea and land.

William Shakespeare *The Taming of the
Shrew*

"

BIRD BRAINS

More than 90% of **bird** species are monogamous, breeding with only one member of the opposite sex during the mating season. Some of them are perennially monogamous, faithful to the same partner for life. Some are seasonal companions, coming together in the breeding season but living separate lives for the rest of the year and in this group are many migrant birds which return to exactly the same nesting places year after year, meeting up with the same partner. Isn't that sweet? Well, maybe – no one is quite sure whether they really do seek out last year's mate deliberately or whether both male and female are simply loyal to the old nesting site and just happen to find each other on the spot!

Kittiwakes are often faithful to each other for many years – a pair in northern England, for example, were recorded as breeding with each other for 16 years in succession. But although the majority of kittiwakes return to their previous mate at the familiar nesting site, about one in four choose a new partner even if the familiar original mate is present in the breeding colony – these are mainly birds whose eggs had failed to hatch the previous year.

A pair of **mollymawks** (Buller's albatrosses) which were first noted breeding together in 1948 were still producing young together in 1971.

In monogamous bird species, the male often helps his mate to care for the eggs and the hatched young. In fact, in about 50% of all bird species they share incubation duties, changing shifts perhaps every few hours or, in the case of **penguins** and some other seabirds, after many days while the other partner has been stocking up on food at sea. In 6% of all species, the male does all the incubating.

The **ostrich**, the **rhea**, the **cassowary** and the **tinamou** are closely related species and throughout the group the female lays the eggs but thereafter the male takes charge. The male tinamou, for example, incubates the eggs himself and then keeps a fatherly eye on the young when they have hatched. The male ostrich is not quite so modern: he only incubates the eggs at night, while the dominant female takes the day shift, and the nest sometimes contains the eggs of less dominant females as well.

Button quail fathers are wholly responsible for the brooding and rearing of the young. In some **woodpecker** species, too, only the males take care of the young and the same is true of **wood swallows** in Australia. And then there is the extraordinary **mound-builder** – it is the male who builds the huge compost-heap of rotting vegetation for egg incubation, and he controls its temperature right through to hatching time by carefully removing or adding vegetation as necessary.

Cockatiels carefully share incubation duties – the male sits on the eggs during the day and the female at night. **Pigeons**, too, take turns on the nest (the male sits on a four-hour afternoon shift, for example, but it is always the mum on the night shift). They feed their young on 'milk', a specially rich substance regurgitated by both parents. Pigeons pair for life and are strictly monogamous: if you put a random group of young pigeons together, they will form pairs within ten days and the bonds last for a lifetime.

Someone once tested a large group of **barbary doves**: the birds were allotted partners by the experimenter and allowed to mate and rear the first batch of young. Then they were separated for eight months to see if they would recognise each other in a crowd. They all passed the test with flying(!) colours – without exception each chose to mate again with the original partner, rejecting all the others.

Swans, **field geese** and **cranes** tend to be monogamous for life, and they continue to associate with their partners whether or not it is the breeding season. Thousands of **Bewick swans** visit the Slimbridge Wildfowl Trust in Gloucestershire every year and never once have observers recorded a 'divorce' among the pairs, although very occasionally a 'widowed' bird will take a new mate. Otherwise they are faithful until death.

African **violet-eared waxbills** establish monogamous partnerships by the time they are 35 days old and are still being fed by their parents. Some **lovebirds** form pairs when they are only two months old and still wearing their juvenile plumage.

Some bird species are polygamous, having perhaps two or three mates, either at the same time or one after another. Very few of these species are polyandrous (where the female has more than one mate) but most are polygynous (the male has several mates).

Some, like **pheasants** and domestic **chickens**, are harem birds – the cock gathers about him a whole group of hens and mates with as many as possible, trying to persuade them that his territory is the best for miles around. It is to the female's advantage if the male in a polygynous species has a large territory with a choice of good nesting sites and plenty of food – this is more of a bonus than a faithful and helpful 'housefather'. Cock pheasants take no part at all in incubating the eggs or looking after the young – they are much too busy keeping the harem in order, showing off, protecting their hens and arguing with other cocks about their territorial boundaries.

Ruffs and **black grouse** all mate within a limited area known as a 'lek'. The males compete furiously for territories within the lek, especially for the favourite central part of the area, and the females noticeably prefer males with central territories. They choose mates who offer a suitable balance of territorial dominance (a demonstration of the male's fitness and strength) with the submissive displays that prove courtship maturity – no toyboys in the lek, thanks!

Other species are totally promiscuous in that birds of both sexes mate at random with one or more of the opposite sex, without forming any pair bonds. The American **jacana** is unusual among birds in that the females are more showy and dominant than the males – they are territorial and actively court the males. When a female has successfully laid her first clutch of eggs, it is then incubated solely by the male while she minces off to find herself another mate for another clutch to be incubated by the new housefather, so that she can go off again and find another, and then another . . . Meanwhile, the little jacanas are cared for entirely by the male, and the same is true of the **painted snipe** and the **phalarope** species.

Before all these parental burdens, of course, there is the business of attracting a mate in the first place. Birds rely largely on two senses: sight and hearing. Many males have flashy plumage to draw attention to themselves, and they show it off in various ways to attract females. The male **lapwing**, for example, displays his eye-catching black-and-white coat in a soaring and tumbling courtship flight which advertises his splendour up to a considerable distance.

Song is another way of advertising and **nightingales** and **nightjars** take advantage of the stillness of the night to attract passing females vocally. The nightingale's rich and beautiful singing is legendary; the nightjar prefers a loud, chirring purr. Better than a human serenade under the balcony by moonlight . . .

Drakes use a combination of colourful plumage and posturing displays to demonstrate their masculinity and identify their species for the ducks, who are often drab-feathered and rather alike in appearance. Some waterfowl are quite gorgeous but some of their displays, to the human eye at least, make them look rather ridiculous! Others are more elegant – the mandarin drake, who looks like a painting-by-numbers come to life, includes the delicate little gesture of pointing the tip of his beak towards a particularly brilliant orange wing feather, rather like a dandy drawing attention to his dazzling jewellery.

Peacock males are famous show-offs, strutting about as if they were on the catwalk, fanning and quivering their huge tailcoverts with the multitude of 'evil eyes'. The **sage grouse** is another male posturer with dramatic display plumage, and all the male **pheasants**, often beautifully coloured, try to make themselves look as big as possible when on display by puffing out their feathers all along one side. They also offer their hens little titbits – or, rather, they draw attention to real or imaginary morsels, picking them up and carefully putting them down again, with a special sound designed to tempt the hens closer.

Charles Darwin believed that, in most cases for most species, it is the female who chooses the male from the potential mates available. It is usually she who invests most heavily in the production of offspring whether 'she' is a bird, a mammal or a bug, and she has the right to be choosy about the quality of her mate. Males are often more interested in quantity than quality!

Blackheaded gulls have a problem. Their dark face-masks, present on both sexes, automatically trigger aggressive responses in each other, so during courtship they turn their faces away. They also indulge in courtship feeding – the female appeases the male by behaving like a juvenile and begging for food, which he magnanimously regurgitates for her.

Chaffinches are beset by indecision in courtship. Outside the breeding season males use a threat posture against other chaffinches of either sex, if food is in dispute. A male's initial courtship display to a female is similar at first but a little less threatening, as if he were not quite sure whether to chase her off or to skedaddle himself. The closer he comes to her, the more submissive and timid his posture. And immediately after he has succeeded in mating with her, he flies off with the standard alarm-call of 'Watch it – there's a hawk coming!'

Male **flicker** birds have black 'moustache' stripes which differentiate them from females. If you were to catch the female of a pair and give her a false moustache, her own mate would promptly attack her as if she were a male rival.

Bower-birds in Australia and New Guinea are master builders. The males create elaborate courtship bowers to attract females and some of these bowers are up to half a metre high and nearly a metre long. They are often maintained by the bird for several years. Most are decorated with a collection of attractive objects – shiny and brightly coloured things, flowers, small bones, feathers and so on, according to the owner's taste. Some are even painted with a mixture of charcoal or vegetable juices and the bird's saliva. In one bower a bird had collected more than 1300 bones from small mammals (his species is sometimes known as the sepulchre bird); another collected car-keys, and another stole a bushman's glass eye from a cup while he was asleep!

The **pelicans** in St James's Park, London, are ridiculously shy – they never breed. There have been pelicans in the park since James I created the waterfowl collection there, but none has ever laid an egg and the population can only be maintained by gifts of new pelicans from overseas.

Flamingoes in captivity have the same problem – like pelicans, they mate in the wild in huge flocks

and seem to become self-conscious in smaller groups. Some zoos are now carrying out experiments to ease the birds' embarrassment – it's all done with mirrors, which are supposed to fool the birds into believing that they are part of a crowd.

ANIMAL LOVERS

Mammals and other animal groups, unlike birds, are much more likely to be polygamous than monogamous. A female mammal devotes much time and energy to rearing her young, while the male equally spends much time and energy in spreading his genes! There are, however, faithful exceptions. **Wolves**, for example, generally have one partner for life and are known to mourn if that partner dies (some never mate again). **Dogs** have been somewhat debased by their relationship with humans and, as every dog-owner knows, male dogs will happily mate with any bitch who happens to be in season.

Some species lead essentially solitary lives, only getting together for transitory mating. They include small arboreal and nocturnal insectivores like **lemurs**, **loris** and **tarsiers**, and also many of the mustelids like **polecats** and **ferrets**. **Primates** are usually much more sociable – some exist in small groups, which often have a dominant male (as with the **mountain gorilla**) or several males (as with olive and yellow **baboons**). The **white-handed gibbon** is an example of a monogamous primate but the **hamadryas baboon** is polygamous: a young male gathers a harem of females long before he is adult and he will even kidnap female infants from their mothers. Although they might be two or three years too young for mating, he 'adopts' them into his harem as 'just good friends' and spends much time cuddling and grooming them and playing.

Flo was the queen chimpanzee in the Gombe Stream Reserve in Tanzania where Jane van Lawick-Goodall began studying these wild primates in 1960. Scrawny Flo was no beauty – she had a bulbous nose and a torn ear – but none of the adult males could resist her charms when she was ready to mate and they even queued up for the privilege!

Humpback whales use song to communicate. Their sounds range from the deepest imaginable rumbling, like an undersea cathedral organ, to the highest bat-like squeaks and there are probably frequencies beyond these extremes which the human ear cannot detect. The song is very loud indeed and can be transmitted over long distances underwater, especially within certain strata known as 'sound tunnels' under the ocean. In theory, such a whale's song could travel around the underwater world and be heard by another whale thousands of miles away. Well, it's a lot cheaper than a lover's telephone call!

Frogs and **toads**, like pelicans and flamingoes, need to get together in large crowds so that they can locate a mate. They congregate in huge numbers at traditional breeding ponds when the time is right but the problem is finding a member of the opposite sex in the crowd. European male toads simply clasp other toads indiscriminately, male or female, but if another male is groped he immediately makes a certain call (probably 'Ger'off!') and is released.

In some species of amphibian, it is the male who guards the eggs. The male **midwife toad** carries around with him a great mass of fertilised eggs, wrapped like a girdle around his waist, and he carefully chooses exactly the right conditions of humidity and temperature for their development. Just before they hatch, he returns to the pond and lets the little tadpoles emerge in the water. A male **South American frog** guards his mate's eggs and, shortly before hatching time, he eats them: one by one he carefully takes the eggs into his mouth and stores them in his vocal sac, carrying them there until they hatch and then the fully developed tadpoles emerge from his mouth.

Pacific tree frogs congregate in masses in ponds and the males all join in a loud chorus. Each is intent on singing continuously for longer than the others and eventually only one will still be making music. The females, who begin to move in as the chorus dwindles, all make for the winner.

Male **fence lizards** bob their heads rhythmically to attract females. Some related species are rather similar and, to avoid confusing the girls, each species bobs at characteristically different rates.

A male **smooth newt** initially meets a female at random as he wanders about in the breeding pond but thereafter he leaves nothing to chance, setting out to attract her by sight, smell and touch. In an elaborate ritual of courtship he shows off his brilliant colours and patterns, then fans his broad tail in the water to waft his smell towards her and also to send vibrating currents to tickle her fancy. She acts shy, feigning indifference for a while and swimming away when he tries to place himself right in front of her less than admiring eyes. Eventually she falls for his splendid good looks, becoming increasingly reluctant to swim away (or does she simply get fed up with trying to evade such pushy behaviour?). However, it is a long and complicated ritual dance, which takes place at the bottom of the pond so that, every now and then, one or other partner must break off the sequence and escape to the surface to snatch a quick gulp of fresh air!

The Egyptian **ghost crab** digs a sand burrow and advertises it to potential mates by building up the excavated sand into a visible pyramid nearby. The male **fiddler crab** has a grossly enlarged claw which he waves rhythmically while he 'dances' in his courtship display – a clear case of 'come and get me . . .'

Another courtship dancer is the **three-spined stickleback**. In this species, the male rather than the female devotes most of his time and energy to rearing the babies while she is much less coy during courtship than many other fish. The dance follows a deliberate sequence of actions by each partner and neither will proceed to the next move until there has been an appropriate response to the previous one. They keep in step throughout, like synchronised swimmers, or give up the whole idea. If the female *does* respond, the male leads her to the nest he has made and encourages her to lay eggs in it.

The male **bullhead** fish has no time for such civilities. He simply lies in wait in his burrow and rushes out to grab any passing female, taking her head in his jaws. Only those ready to mate react submissively and let him drag them by the head into his lair. Others will quickly wriggle free: when a bullhead lady says no, she means it.

Male **sea-horses** carry their mates' eggs in special temporary pouches until they hatch.

CREEPY CRAWLIES

Spiders have difficulties. In many species, the female is larger than the male and more likely to eat him than mate with him! He must therefore either lull or ambush her. The male **jumping spider** attracts the female's attention by waving a semaphore message with his legs from a very safe distance and only comes closer if she responds with a clear invitation. A **garden spider** twangs rhythmically at a far corner of the female's web, plucking to a precise pattern, and he too only ventures towards her if she responds favourably. Others are crafty – the male **wolf spider** offers a gift of food wrapped in silk – and then mates with the female while she is busy unwrapping the parcel and eating the contents. Other species use brute force, tying down their mates with silken threads before attempting to mate, and the males of one species have special devices with which they can lock the female's mouth open so that she cannot possibly eat while she is mated!

Emphid flies are balloonists. The males make themselves hollow silk balloons as big as their own bodies and then a whole group of balloon-wavers display collectively to a visiting group of females. When a female chooses one of the males, she accepts the gift of his balloon as a sign that she is willing to mate with him.

Fruit flies are well known to genetics students as they are widely used in breeding experiments. It pays a male fruit fly to be different – he is more likely to attract a female if he looks unusual. The females are highly selective in choosing a mate but the males are indiscriminate. As well as looking different, the male also 'sings' to his mate by vibrating his wings, and the same wingbeats waft his pheromones towards her.

Pheromones are organic molecules with five to 20 carbon atoms. They are chemical substances secreted for use as signals, sending out messages into the surrounding air or water, or deposited deliberately on solid objects. The small molecules are used as alarm signals and the larger ones as sexual attractants. The females of many **moth** species attract the opposite sex by wafting pheromones on the breeze so that the males can find them by smell. A male **silk moth's** antennae are so sensitive that he can detect female pheromones from a source several miles away.

Male **firefly** beetles attract mates by flashing a sort of morse code. The female responds to a code appropriate to her own species by waiting for a deliberate length of time before flashing a reply of specific duration. Only if her code is correct will the male gradually approach in response to her repeated signals. But he must be careful – in one species the female's intention is to eat males of several other species and she lures them with a false code of flashes.

Male **tree crickets** attract mates by 'singing' – they rub their forewings together to create a sound. Each species has its specific song and the females react only to the song-pattern of their own species. The songs are issued as a series of rapid pulses and the females can distinguish between the different pulse rates of different species even when all types increase in rate during warm weather. Other **crickets** and **cicadas** 'sing' in a similar way to attract females. **Grasshoppers** make their music by rubbing their hindlegs against their abdomens.

CREATURE FEATURES
Well-known panda partners:
Kan Kan and Lan Lan
An An and Chi Chi
Hsing Hsing and Ling Ling – the former proved inept so she was introduced to Chia Chia, and they promptly had a mighty fistfight. It is notoriously difficult to mate pandas successfully in captivity. The artificial insemination of Juan Juan at Beijing Zoo resulted in the birth of Yuanjing in 1978.

Animal 'couples' from the Silver Screen:
Lady and the Tramp: *she* was a pretty spaniel, tormented by some visiting Siamese cats; *he* was the raffish street mutt who loved her and led her on some wild escapades.
Mickey Mouse and Minnie: they first appeared in 1928 in Walt Disney's *Steamboat Willie*. He once smuggled her out of a harem disguised as a potted plant. On another occasion, he kissed her in a plane and she angrily parachuted out suspended by her bloomers!
Miss Piggy and Kermit the Frog: she is the glamorous and 'supremely talented' pig whose beauty is her curse, and he is the muppet who does not return her passion. Kermit was created way back in 1956 but did not become a star for another 20 years, wincing at the thought of any 'involvement' with the amorous Miss P.

love me, love my dog!

PROVERBS

Love . . . begets love
is blind
laughs at locksmiths
makes the world go round
will find a way
and a cough cannot be hid

Love me, **love** my dog

Love me little, **love** me long

One cannot **love** and be wise

The course of true **love** never did run smooth

All's fair in **love** and war

Lucky at cards, unlucky in **love**

Off with the old **love** before on with the new

Pity is akin to **love**

When poverty comes in at the door, **love** flies out of the window

'Tis better to have **loved** and lost than never to have **loved** at all

The quarrel of lovers is the renewal of **love**

Kissing goes by favour

When the gorse is out of bloom, **kissing**'s out of fashion

When the furze is in bloom, my **love**'s in tune

Marriage is a lottery

Marriages are made in heaven

There goes more to **marriage** than four bare legs in a bed

Marry in haste, repent at leisure

One **wedding** brings another

Better **wed** over the mixen than over the moor (ie better to marry a neighbour than a stranger)

Happy is the **bride** that the sun shines on

My son is my son till he gets him a **wife**,
But my daughter's my daughter all the days of her life

If you would be happy for a week, take a **wife**

He that will thrive must first ask his **wife**

A deaf **husband** and a blind **wife** are always a happy couple

The word 'husband' comes from the Old Norse words *hus* (house) and *boa* (to dwell) – ie one who has a household. The origin of the word 'wife' is uncertain. Possibly, it is derived from the Old Norse *vifathr*, meaning 'veiled'.

PORTRAIT OF A MARRIAGE

Marriage is such an important part of life that it inevitably features in numerous works of art.

The **Aldobrandini Wedding** was found on the wall of a Roman mansion – it shows a miserable-looking bride dressed in white, with a white drape over her head, being consoled by Venus, the Roman goddess of love, while her mother and attendants prepare her prenuptial bath.

The **Arnolfini Marriage** was painted by the 15th-century Flemish artist Jan van Eyck. It shows Giovanni di Arrigo Arnolfini, a merchant from Lucca, with Giovanna Cenami, the daughter of another Luccan merchant who lived in Paris. The picture, painted at Bruges, shows their marriage taking place at a period when couples could contract marriage without the presence of a priest – they simply married by mutual consent, using appropriate words and actions. As in similar love paintings, the little dog (a griffon) represents fidelity, and the single candle is a marriage candle.

The **Mystic Marriage of St Catherine**, painted by Parmigianino (1503–1540) shows St Catherine of Alexandria undergoing her mystic marriage with Christ. She gave her name to the well-known Catherine wheel firework – she was martyred on a spiked wheel.

Jacob Jordaens (1593–1678) painted a typical marriage picture, thought to be of **Govaert van Surpele** and his wife though their identity is not

Hendrickje Stoffels was the mistress of Rembrandt (1606–1669) and a frequent subject of his paintings. His wife had died several years before the couple became lovers, and in the terms of her will he would have to give up half the estate if he remarried – which is probably why Hendrickje remained his mistress, not his wife. She was summoned by the Reform Church Council to be admonished for living in sin and, later the same year, gave birth to Rembrandt's daughter. Four years later the artist was declared bankrupt and in due course Hendrickje and his son, Titus, 'employed' him to protect him from his creditors.

certain. Van Surpele married twice, and both wives were called Catarina. The picture shows the couple in middle age and she is decidedly plump. There is a dog in the scene.

A Man and Woman Beside a Virginal, by Gabriel Metsu (1629–1667) is a typical 17th-century Dutch courtship scene – musical instruments were a traditional feature. Johannes Vermeer (1632–1675) painted **A Young Woman Standing at a Virginal** as an illustration in praise of fidelity to one man as opposed to the love of many. Cupid is shown in a picture on the young girl's wall. The virginal is a spinet-like keyboard instrument, a favourite with young ladies in times gone by, and the symbolism is obvious.

The **Marriage of Frederick Barbarossa and Beatrice of Burgundy** was painted by Giovanni Domenico Tiepolo (1727–1804). He had to use his imagination – the marriage of the German Emperor had taken place at Würzburg in 1156!

Marriage à la Mode, by William Hogarth (1697–1764) is a satirical series of six pictures on contemporary high life and marriage based on money and vanity. The first is **The Marriage Contract**, where the couple, soon to be fettered like the symbolic dogs in front of them, are expressing little interest in each other. The girl is paying much more attention to Counsellor Silvertongue, whose subsequent affair with her eventually leads to disaster. In this first picture, her wealthy father is negotiating the marriage contract with the bridegroom's noble but gouty father, Lord Squander – money is marrying class. The second picture, **Shortly After the Marriage**, reveals that the young husband (a Viscount) is already being unfaithful and Cupid, pictured playing the bagpipes, mocks the loveless marriage. In the next, **The Visit to the Quack Doctor**, the Viscount is merrily taking his very young mistress to see the doctor about venereal disease. The fourth is **The Countess's Morning Levee** – the wife is now a titled woman but is ignoring all her guests except Silvertongue the lawyer. In the fifth, **The Killing of the Earl**, the husband has been killed by Silvertongue when he discovers him with the Countess. The final scene, **The Suicide of the Countess**, shows her in a squalid, poverty-stricken room, reading a statement that Silvertongue has been hanged for murdering the Earl.

The Marriage of Giovanni Arnolfini and Giovanna Cenami *by Van Eyck (d. 1441).*

Right: Wedded *painted in 1882 by the distinguished painter and sculptor, Frederic, First Baron Leighton (1830–1896). It was one of several of his pictures to become a massive best-seller. It was reproduced in thousands by photogravure techniques. However, Leighton, the son of a Scarborough doctor, never married.*

Left: The Mystic Marriage of St Catherine *by Parmigianino (1503–1540).*

YE OLDE ENGLISHE WYFE

In **Anglo-Saxon** England there was a **class system** which included 'unfree' groups – slave Britons, penal slaves bonded in punishment for certain crimes, and prisoners taken during wars between the various English kingdoms. Apparently it was not uncommon for people to be captured as slaves and, in his *Penitential* (c 672), **Archbishop Theodore** found it necessary to allow anyone whose husband or wife had been put into captivity, and could not be redeemed, to remarry after five years if they wished, just as if they had been widowed. The wife of a penal slave could remarry after only one year.

As the Christian Church gained strength in Anglo-Saxon England, it began taking measures to forbid **divorce** and also to restrict marriage between certain degrees of kinship. **Pope Gregory I** allowed marriage within the 3rd or 4th degree of kinship but in due course it became forbidden within the 6th degree, or between widows or widowers of kinsmen within the same degree. Earlier, **Wihtred** of Kent had prohibited illicit marriages – he would not allow into his country any foreigners so married. Four centuries later **Cnut** agreed on this matter when he was trying to clean up the morals of Scandinavian settlers in England.

In particular the Church objected to a man marrying his own **stepmother**, a Germanic practice carried out by **King Eadbald** of Kent when his father Ethelbert died in 616, and by **Aethelbald** in the 9th century who married **Judith**, a Frankish princess who as a child had been married to his most pious father **King Aethelwulf**, though the latter had failed to consummate the marriage.

Divorce was much simpler in early Kentish law. A wife who wished to 'depart with her children' could take half the household goods with her. If her husband wanted to keep the children, she was allowed a share of goods equal to that of a child.

In Durham in the 11th century, an earl divorced two wives in quick succession so that he could marry a more noble third; his first wife gaily married again, and divorced again. In the same province, two brothers shared a wife until the archbishop lost his patience and fined them a whole estate. But even the **Domesday Book** mentions separation and divorce quite casually – clearly divorce is not a modern disease.

Kentish men thought of marriage as **wife-purchase**. Their laws said: 'If a freeman lie with the wife of a freeman, he shall pay his wergeld, and get another wife with his own money and bring her to the other man's home.' Hmm. And the laws of Ine stated more poetically: 'A king shall buy a queen with property, with goblets, and bracelets.' Women actually had high status in Anglo-Saxon society and the brideprice was regarded as the bride's own property – a payment made by a suitor 'in order that she might accept his suit'. But women were not to be bought so easily and, even before the Normans were clambering into their cross-Channel ships, the law stated firmly: 'No woman or maiden shall ever be forced to marry one whom she dislikes, nor be sold for money.'

The **'morning-gift'** – a husband's present to his new wife the day after their marriage had been consummated – was entirely her property. She could keep it after her husband's death, whether it was a simple personal adornment or a country estate, but she had to forfeit it if she married again within the year. If she died before her spouse, the morning-gift was inherited by her own kinsfolk rather than being returned to her husband. A **widow** also had the right to a certain proportion of her late husband's household goods (usually a third, although this varied from region to region) but, again, these were forfeited if she remarried 'too soon'. An upper-class woman, however, regarded all the household furnishing as her own

The Anglo-Saxon marriage had two parts. First came the **wedding**, which was the betrothal or pledging. At this stage the brideprice was paid and the terms of the marriage drawn up and agreed. Then came the **gift** where the bride was given to the groom, with much ceremony and feasting. The marriage was then considered legal, whether or not it had been blessed by the Church.

'I would,' said William Powell in 1631, on the subject of wives, 'have their breeding like to the Dutch woman's clothing tending to profit only and comeliness.' His opinion was that wives should prefer sewing, cooking and laundering to fancy dancing and musicianship, and he would rather they read *Grounds of Good Huswifery* than novels of poetry.

and could bequeath it as she wished in her own will. However, all this female power was to disappear after the Norman Conquest.

As for the wife of a **thief**, she was not held responsible for any stolen property found in her home (unless she herself had locked it away) because she was bound to obey her husband and could not stop him bringing whatever he pleased into the house. If he was actually convicted of theft, he forfeited his property but she retained her due share.

After the Norman Conquest, William's barons became **lords** who held land in return for service to their king. With the land they assumed a lord's control and rights over all who happened to live within their boundaries. For example, they controlled the marriages of heirs of their deceased tenants. The lord could 'sell' the heir's gift in marriage – unless he had a female relation in need of a husband. The lord could also profit from the widow of a military tenant (she possessed a third of her late husband's land and would make a good match for somebody) or the lord could demand from her a proportion of her financial resources in exchange for her right to marry another man of her choice, or indeed to choose to remain unmarried.

King John (1167–1216) preferred the Anglo-Saxon idea that widows should not be forced to marry again but, until then, even the greatest of ladies was bound to give money or else remarry according to the king's whim. For example, **Richard I** (1157–99) forced **Hawisa**, Countess of Aumale and widow of the Earl of Essex, to marry **William de Forz** of Poitou (a man of much lower social status than she) or to give him all her goods.

Post-Conquest daughters who were not heiresses were in trouble. They needed marriage portions to wed and even the alternative of becoming a nun required some endowment. However, if the girl was the daughter of a tenant of a great lord who had many dependent knights, he might marry her off to one of them, but only if the lord was first prepared to attract the knight into such a marriage by means of some provision. For example, the **Earl of Warwick** gave his own daughter, **Alice**, in marriage to the king's chamberlain, **Geoffrey of Glympton**, who held 17 knights' fees of the earl. Alice's father reduced the number of knights owed to him by ten to make the idea of marriage more attractive to Geoffrey. Another lord, **Gilbert de Gant**, of Lincolnshire, made similar concessions to secure the marriage of his daughter **Juliana** to **Geoffrey**, son of **Henry de Armentiers**. He also paid Geoffrey's knightly expenses, paid Henry 60 marks, and found a manor for the young couple's new home. One wonders what was so unappealing about Juliana that so much inducement was needed!

In the Middle Ages, when **land ownership** was every man's aim, marriage was seen as the easiest way of grabbing unearned wealth. It was considered strictly a business matter. Heiresses often found themselves being married off as small

The 17th-century diarist John Evelyn said that, in his youth, wives were chosen 'for their Modesty, Frugality, keeping at home, Good Housekeeping and other Oeconomical Virtues then in Reputation; and when the young Damsels were taught all these in the Country, and their Parents Houses, the Portion they brought was more in Virtue than in Money. The Presents which were made when all was concluded, were a Ring, a Necklace of Pearl, and perhaps another fair Jewel, the Bona Paraphernalia of her prudent Mother whose Nuptual Kirtle, Gown and Petticoat lasted as many Anniverseries as the happy Couple lived together . . .'

A Frenchwoman wrote in *Country-Ferme* in early Stuart times: 'The condition and state of a huswife is that countrie women looke unto things necessarie and requisite about kine, calves, hogs, pigs, pigeons, geese, duckes, peacockes, hennes, feasants, and other sorts of beasts, as well for the feeding of them as for the milking of them: making of butter and cheese; and the keeping of lard to dresse the labouring men their vittails withal. Yet furthermore they have the charge of the oven and cellar; and we leave the handling of hempe unto them likewise; as also the care of making of webs, of looking to the clipping of sheepe, of keeping their fleeces, of spinning and combing of wooll to make cloth to cloath the familie, of ordring of the kitchen garden; and keeping of the fruites, herbes, rootes and seedes, and moreover of watching and attending the bees. Buying and selling and paying of wages belongeth to the man. But the surplussage to be imploied and laid out in pettie matters, as in linnens, cloathes for the household, and all necessaries of household furniture, that of a certaintie belongeth unto the women.'

A book written in 1672 (*The Office of the Good Housewife*) repeats all these wifely duties and adds to them the care of silkworms, muckspreading and ploughing.

children – for example, **Galiena de Damartin** was only seven years old at her first marriage (she had three husbands in all).

Elizabeth Howland, daughter of **Sir John Howland** of Essex and Surrey (a city draper), married when she was 13. Her husband **Wriothesley Child**, only 14½ himself, was the son of clothier **Sir Josiah Child**, chairman of the East India Company. After the elaborate wedding ceremony in 1695, the couple parted and only met occasionally – Elizabeth lived with her mother while her husband took a grand tour abroad with his tutor. It was quite common for 17th-century girls to be married between the ages of 13 and 18 to young men between 15 and 28, chosen by the girls' parents, and these arranged marriages often turned out well – as long as the girl brought sufficient wealth into the marriage.

Hannah Woolley, the 17th-century author of books on preserving, cooking, and the art of being a gentlewoman, did not agree with the idea that men were superior. In 1675 she wrote: 'Vain man is apt to think we were merely intended for the world's propagation and to keep its humane inhabitants sweet and clean; but by their leaves had we the same literature he would find our brains as fruitful as our bodies.' Hannah had been a schoolmistress at the age of 14, in sole charge of her little school.

MARRIAGE FACTS

Seven out of ten people in **Britain** get married at some time in their lives, and seven out of ten first marriages take place in a church.

The third quarter of each year is definitely the most popular time for marriages in all parts of the UK.

In 1987, the UK and Portugal had the highest marriage rates (marriages per 1000 of the eligible population) in the European Community, while France had the lowest. In 1981, Britain had been third to Portugal and Greece, and Denmark had the lowest marriage rate.

There were about 394 000 marriages in Britain in 1988 – about the same as in 1981 and 1961, but in 1971 the figure dropped by 14%.

In the UK, 64% of all marriages in 1988 were between bachelors and spinsters, but in 1961 the figure was 86%.

The number of first marriages, for men and for

UK Marriages (by 1000s) 1983–88

	ENGLAND	WALES	SCOTLAND	N. IRELAND	UK TOTAL
1983	324.4	19.9	35.0	10.0	389.3
1984	330.0	19.2	36.3	10.4	395.8
1985	327.3	19.1	36.4	10.3	393.1
1986	328.4	19.5	35.8	10.2	393.9
1987	332.3	19.5	35.8	10.4	397.9
1988	329.2	19.3	35.6	10.0	394.1

women, per 1000 population has fallen since 1971. For women aged less than 20 the rate has dropped by three-quarters and for men the rate has dropped by two-thirds.

The ratio by age has changed: in 1961, the most spinsters were in the 20–24 age group, but in 1988 the most were among the 25–29s. Among bachelors, however, the highest rate remains in the 25–29 age group.

Those in ethnic minorities in Britain are in general more likely to be single than whites, but far more white women are likely to be divorced. White men are the most likely to be married (52%) and the figure is the same for Indian women in Britain, while Africans and West Indians are the most likely to be divorced or separated.

The proportion of remarriages (ie where one or both partners have been married before) was 36% in 1988 – 132 000 marriages that year involved at least one divorced partner (compared with 34 000 in 1961) and 18 000 involved a widow or widower (29 000 in 1961).

During the 1960s and early 1970s, the remarriage rate for divorced or widowed men increased rapidly, peaking in 1972 (which was the year after the Divorce Reform Act 1969 came into force in England and Wales) at nearly 88 per 1000 population. It has since fallen back to the mid-1960s rate which is 50 per 1000 population.

In 1988–89, 26.4% of women aged 18–49 were cohabiting (ie living with a man without being legally married to him). The largest proportion was in the 18–24 age group. In 1979, the figure was only 9.4%. Among men, 13% of the 25–29 age group were cohabiting in 1988–89.

A major study of **American** husbands and wives was issued in 1978 by the US Bureau of

> *When a man marries a woman, he promises to love, comfort and honour her, to keep her in sickness and in health, and to worship her with his body. Nowhere in the marriage contract is a husband permitted to beat his wife (or she him). Yet for centuries some men have assumed that violence within a marriage is more permissible than outside it . . .*
>
> Leading article in *The Times*, 1st August, 1990

> *Falling in love is a two-way street – so is falling out of it.*
>
> Barbara Amiel, journalist, May 1990

> *Cuckoo, cuckoo, – O word of fear Unpleasing to a married ear!*
>
> William Shakespeare *Love's Labour's Lost*

> *How can a couple sign a contract to be faithful for the rest of their lives when they do not know the hidden clauses?*
>
> Lee Rodwell, journalist, 1990

Census. It noted the following facts:

Only 6% of men and 4% of women in their early 50s had never married.

Eighty-five per cent of married men and 88% of married women had been married only once.

About 1% of all married couples were inter-racial, an increase of a third between 1970 and 1978.

Husbands and wives tended to have similar levels of education.

In only about one in six couples did both spouses work in year-round full-time jobs. The median income for dual-income couples in 1976 was $17570, and in one in three cases the wife's earnings were equal to, or greater than, the hus-band's.

Each American state has its own laws regarding legal minimum age for marriage, and other condi-tions. Ten years ago the legal minimum age for marriage without parental consent in most states was 18, except for Nebraska and Wyoming (19), Montana and Utah (16), and Minnesota, Missis-sippi and New York (21). In Georgia, however, a girl could marry at any age if she gave proof of pregnancy, signed by a physician, or if she was mar-rying the father of a child born out of wedlock.

In the late 1970s, the highest number of mar-riages took place in Texas, California, New York and Nevada. Nevada's population is far from dense but its divorce and remarriage laws at the time were exceptionally free.

The American median age at first marriage has changed over the years. In 1890, it was 26.1 for men and 22.0 for women. For men, it gradually but consistently dropped over the decades to 22.8

> **"**
>
> *The potential for an affair is there in any relationship, it is built in from the start. It is commonly held that those who have the affair are those who create it. But the triangle does not consist of two guilty lovers and their victims: all three people involved, whether they are aware of it or not, create what happens.*
>
> Susan Quilliam *The Eternal Triangle*
>
> **"**

in 1960, but it then began to rise again and stood at 24.5 by 1980. For women, the pattern was less consistent but there was an overall drop to 20.3 in 1950 and 1960, and since then it has been slowly rising. It was back to 22 by 1980 and is still going up.

In 1900, the rate of marriage in the US was 9.3 per thousand of the eligible population and 709000 marriages took place. In 1920 and 1940, the rate was 12.0 and 12.1 (1274476 and 1595879 marriages respectively) but in 1960, it crashed down to 8.5, with only 1523000 mar-riages – the rate was particularly low from 1958 to 1962. Throughout the 1970s, the rate remained fairly steady at about 10.5. The record rate was immediately after the Second World War – it was 16.4 in 1946, when there were 2291045 mar-riages – a number not exceeded until the 1970s.

In 1900 only 0.9% of American men aged 14–19 had ever been married, compared with 9.4% of girls of the same age group, whereas 89.7% of men aged 45–54 and 92.2% of women of that age had married at some time in their lives. In 1960, though the marriage rates were at an all-time low, the number of men who had ever married, reached an all-time peak of 3.3% in the youngest age group, whereas the percentage for girls of that age had fallen to 13.5% from a high of 14.4% in 1950. Then, very dramatically, in 1979 the figure for girls aged 14–19, who had ever been married, crashed to only 1.2%, though 95.6% of women aged 45–54 had married at some stage.

In 1960, 41% of those who lived alone were aged 64 or more; the number of singles in the 14–24 age group had leapt from 3.3% to 9.4% by 1979. In 1980, there were nearly twice as many one-parent families maintained by women as in 1960, with the sharpest increases in the divorced group and among the under-35s.

INFIDELITY

St Thomas Aquinas (1225–1274) said that divine law forbade fornication because the father should stay with the mother while the children were being reared, since he was more rational in the children's education and had more physical strength to punish their misdemeanours. He believed that polygyny was unfair to women, and that polyandry cast doubts on the paternity of the

The Revolutionist's Bride *(1799) from the painting by F.H. Karenhmerer.*

children. Incest was forbidden because it complicated family life.

A **cuckold** is a man whose wife is unfaithful. The term is derived from the cuckoo, a bird which lays eggs in other birds' nests, so logically it should be applied to the wife's lover rather than the victim husband. The Romans used to call an adulterer a cuckoo (*cuculum*). However, it came to be used as a word of warning to the husband, as an adulterer approached, but it eventually attached itself to the husband, not the adulterer.

The German equivalent of cuckold is *Hahnrei*, which originally meant a capon (castrated cockerel). It used to be the rather odd practice to graft such a cockerel's spurs to the root of his comb, where they grew into 'horns'.

Near Deptford, on the banks of the River Thames, there is a place known as **Cuckold's Point**. It is said that King John (1167–1216) made love to a labourer's wife there.

Actaeon was a boastful huntsman in Greek mythology, who made the mistake of surprising Artemis, the goddess of the hunt and moon, while she was bathing. She turned him into a stag and he was killed by his own hounds. He became representative, as a stag, of men whose wives were unfaithful. The connection, however, is a little obscure. In the rutting season, a stag gathers several females into his harem but if he is challenged and beaten by another stag he loses his females until he in turn can defeat another. Thus a horned beast has his mates taken from him, and an ancient insulting gesture to a cuckolded husband was to mock him by thrusting up a fist and making 'horns' with the index and little fingers.

The **horn of fidelity** was a magic drinking horn sent to King Arthur. Any woman who was unfaithful to her husband would not be able to drink from it without spilling the contents. King Mark tried it

Recently, an Italian lorry driver visited a local brothel at Teramo to sample the local girls. He had a nasty shock when the manageress opened the door – she was his own scantily-clad wife. He promptly kicked and punched her. Talk about equality!

'Rough music' or 'chivari' is an appalling cacophony created outside the house of someone believed to have committed a marital misdemeanour of some kind – excessive nagging, wife (or husband!) beating, adultery or incest, for example. In some cases the noise treatment is aimed at the victim, rather than the guilty party, for failing in his or her sexual role.

Other names for rough music include riding skimmerton, riding the stag, low-belling, shallal, stag-hunting and hare-hunting. It usually involves three successive nights of loud recitations of the 'crimes' in doggerel verse with much jeering, whistling, shouting, banging of pots and pans, and perhaps the carrying and burning of effigies of the culprit. Often half the village joins in, because of the ancient fears that sexual crimes would bring famine and disaster to the whole tribe. The noise not only shows disapproval but is also supposed to drive off evil demons. Many victims of rough music literally cannot 'face the music' and leave the area forever. Within living memory there was a case of rough music getting out of hand in Liverpool – the adulterer had to be rescued by the police.

out on his queen and a hundred court ladies – only four of them managed to 'drink clean'.

The **Riffians** of North Africa have very strict codes on sexual morality, and a case of adultery will immediately lead the wronged husband to murder or mutilate the man and to nose-snip and banish his faithless wife.

An **Islamic** adulterer is likely to be stoned to death.

During their prolonged absences on the Crusades, untrusting husbands locked their wives into padded, metal **chastity girdles**. There was no equivalent to ensure the faithfulness of husbands – indeed it seems to be quite widespread that wives who have affairs are punished but husbands are not!

In regions as far apart as **Bolivia** and **East Africa**, men suspect infidelity if they are attacked by a wild animal. A hunter who already knows that

Forty years ago, the Kinsey Report, issued by the Kinsey Institute for Research into Sex, Gender and Reproduction, in the USA, revealed that 4 out of 10 American wives were unfaithful. The Institute's latest report, issued in 1990, revealed that the average American age for first sexual intercourse is between 16 and 17, that 4 out of 10 married men are unfaithful (they did not canvass the women this time), that 25% of 'straight' monogamous men had had homosexual experiences and that about half of all failed marriages involved sexual dysfunction.

Henry James Prince (1811–1899) was curate of Charlynch in Somerset. In 1849, he and his rector Samuel Starky founded the Agapemone, or Abode of Love, at Spaxton, where a group of zealots lived communally until their free-love lifestyle led to trouble with the authorities. The movement was revived after 1890 as Children of the Resurrection by one Smyth-Piggott, who was unfrocked in 1909.

his wife has been unfaithful is so convinced of his own disadvantage that he gives up hunting.

The African **Gwambe** tribe of Wutonga believe that the uncleanness of a woman's infidelity must be removed in a series of sexual rites. Even a faithful wife, if she is unsatisfactory in other ways, can be returned to her parents so that the husband can have a refund of the brideprice, or perhaps a substitute wife.

In Africa, a Bantu-speaking **Ngombe** man's first reaction to his wife's adultery is to kill the other man, or at least let him know that his life is in great danger. With luck, the adulterer will live to petition the chief later on so that peace can be negotiated.

A **Hottentot** husband in South West Africa has the right to kill an unfaithful wife.

The recent return of long-time **Iranian prisoners-of-war** from Iraq has had tragic consequences

for some. Many families had to assume that missing soldiers were dead after several years with no news of them and, in keeping with the Islamic custom, their 'widows' have remarried, often under strong family pressure to do so. The wife of missing-presumed-dead soldier Ali, father of her young son, eventually married Ali's brother and they had two children. Their new life was shattered when the government told them in September, 1990, that Ali was in fact alive and about to return from Iraq. The distraught brother, leaving a letter begging fraternal forgiveness, shot himself and died, unaware that Ali (who had been told of the marriage by his uncle) had done exactly the same.

TROUBLE AND STRIFE

For many couples, it is the everyday living together that causes problems, rather than extramarital affairs.

A Scottish husband and wife are sometimes called a **guidman** and **guidwife**, and there is a ballad about one couple called *Get Up and Bar the Door*. The twosome have an argument one night about who should lock the door and huffily decide that the first to speak must do it. Then they sit in determined silence, with the door unbolted, while intruders come in and do as they please, eating the couple's food, shaving off the guidman's beard and kissing the guidwife. Yet still they sit there in silence, neither willing to break the marital deadlock – perhaps this sounds familiar?

The Japanese have invented the '**see you later**' **doll** to keep marriage secure. Japanese employees frequently find themselves spending long periods away from home when their company sends them to its provincial offices and factories, often for several months on end. (Wives are ordered to stay at home to avoid disrupting the children's education.) The lonely husband, miserable in a bedsit, can now take his kneeling, kimono-clad doll with him – she is programmed to respond to a gentle tap on the shoulder by saying demurely, 'See you later.' Some are more conversational and say, invitingly, 'Please hurry back,' 'I'm really going to miss you,' or, in more wifely fashion, 'Don't forget anything.' No doubt an American version would say, 'Have a nice day.' The plastic dolls retail at £15 each and so far 50 000 have been sold.

GOOD BREEDING

In many cultures and religions, the primary function of marriage is the **procreation** of the species and sometimes ludicrous or even desperate measures are taken by a wife who has failed to conceive. These days she can attend a fertility clinic but in the past she would try anything that offered her the faintest hope of bearing a child, and superstitions ran rife.

Some women literally headed for the rocks – or at least for certain magical ones, such as **holestones**, **stone circles** or the flat, bench-like **bedstones** which bore indentations said to show where mythological lovers had lain. Women believed that by coming into contact with these stones they would be made fertile.

At Carnac, in western France, there are prehistoric standing stones (*menhirs*) which childless couples visit by the light of a full moon to make love in the stones' shadows. At Monceaux, in France, the couples sit on the stone 'chair' of St Fiacre, while in Ireland they spend the night on the 'beds' of Diarmid and Grainne. Elsewhere, a barren woman might squeeze through a hole-stone – for example, the **Kelpie Stone** in the River Dee, in Scotland.

In Dorset, the ritual at the village of Cerne Abbas is more concerned with the husband's potency. A man who sits on the graphically well-endowed **Cerne Giant**, a huge figure carved in the turf, will be 'strong'. The Giant is also visited by women who are afraid of losing their husbands or lovers. Other rituals worldwide seek to transfer the virility or fecundity of certain animals to childless couples. This usually involves the wearing or consumption of the animals' testicles.

CALLING IT QUITS

In the 16th and 17th centuries, people whom the church courts had found guilty of **fornication** or **adultery** had to drape themselves in white sheets and stand, holding a candle, to confess their sins in front of a Sunday congregation or a market-square crowd. They were also fined and put in the stocks, or publicly whipped.

During the 18th and 19th centuries, husbands could sue for **damages** from men who had seduced their wives – the accusation was of enjoying 'criminal conversation' (how delicately put!).

A couple living in Colorado Springs had a furious row in 1980 during which the husband, James Searle, slapped his wife's face. She retaliated by jabbing him with a fork. He stormed out to the garage, picked up a tyre iron and struck her with it. Both were arrested and charged with – duelling!

Wives were nonpersons: they were considered as one with their husbands, with no individual identity in law, and therefore could not testify in their own defence if accused of such 'conversation'. **Caroline Norton**, who campaigned for women's rights in the 19th century, was involved in one of these cases, brought by her husband against Lord Melbourne; yet even she said in 1838, 'The natural position of women is inferiority to men. Amen! That is a thing of God's appointing, not of men's devising.'

The year 1799 was a peak time for divorce applications at a period when they were obtained by private petitioning of Parliament – but only ten were actually successful that year, and none were made by women. Over the next four decades only six women made any attempt to petition Parliament for a divorce and only one succeeded. Among the unsuccessful was the unfortunate lady, of very good pedigree, whose bestial and constantly drunken husband had been unfaithful even on their wedding night! He had seduced countless housemaids, passed on a venereal disease to his wife and at the time of her petition he was in prison, his comforts being paid for by a prostitute. Yet the Lord Chancellor of the time said that parliamentary divorce petitions should be allowed only to men, unless something as detestable as incest or bigamy was involved. As late as 1848 a woman's petition for divorce from her husband on the grounds of cruelty and adultery was thrown out by the lords amidst laughter and joking about her claims that he had beaten her with a hairbrush and a riding whip.

Lady Diana Beauclerk, a talented artist and gentlewoman, was the daughter of the second Duke of Marlborough. She had first married Lord

The word *'fornication'* stems from the Latin *fornix*, a brothel or vault, and implies lovemaking between unmarried people. *'Adultery'* comes from *ad alter* ('to another') rather than anything to do with grown-ups, and is the 'violation of the marriage bed (one's own or another's)'.

Bolingbroke, who had treated her appallingly. She was divorced from him in 1768 and two days later married her lover, the dandy Topham Beauclerk, descended from Charles II and Nell Gwynne. Diana was an excellent wife to him but, because she was both a former adulteress and a divorcee, her husband's friend, the lexicographer and prose-writer, Samuel Johnson could without impunity denounce her, saying: 'The woman's a whore, and there's an end on't.' However, James Boswell, the author of *The Life Of Samuel Johnson* (1791) thought highly of her.

The alternative method of release from an impossible situation was by a **private deed of separation** but this was very expensive. It followed that impoverished husbands simply deserted or evicted unwanted wives but a wife could only put up with a rotten marriage or run away – but to where and to what? The most popular way of ending a mutually unwanted marriage was by **unofficial private separation**. Second marriages were not allowed by the ecclesiastical courts, though Parliament could, in special circumstances, grant permission to marry again. It

The fictional Lady Chatterley was not the only upper-class woman to shock her contemporaries by taking a working-class lover. The groom of one John Dormer said of his employer's wife that he had 'lain with her several times' – the wretched Romeo was sued for damages of £5000 – an impossible fortune for a servant to pay.

was not until Prime Minister Palmerston drove his bill through Parliament in 1857 that divorce procedures became a little easier, and it was not until 1923 that women were granted equality with men in seeking divorce on the grounds of their partner's adultery.

Until quite recently, an Englishman's **infidelity** was socially acceptable, or even admirable, but a woman's was quite unforgivable – partly because she ran the risk of pregnancy and might saddle her unwary husband with illegitimate children, but mainly because, as campaigner Caroline Norton had remarked in the 19th century, men were considered superior to women and a wife was the property of her husband. However, in Paris in 1892, a woman called Madame Reymond took matters into her own hands – or, rather, she took a pistol into her own hands and shot her husband's mistress at point-blank range. She used a dagger, too, to make quite sure of her revenge.

In England and Wales the legal concept of divorce dates from the **1753 Marriage Act**. It was the **1969 Divorce Reform Act** which introduced as the solitary ground for divorce the 'irretrievable breakdown' of marriage, which could be established by proving a partner guilty of one of five acts: unreasonable behaviour, adultery, desertion, or living apart for more than five years or for two years. The Act stipulates the five-year separation condition where the partners are not in agreement about the divorce, and the two-year separation if they are in agreement. Moves are in hand to reduce the periods to two years and one year respectively.

The 'fact' most frequently cited in cases where wives have been granted decrees since 1973 is unreasonable behaviour of the husband (in more than half the cases by 1986). However, husbands

British and American birth rates are almost the same, but more than two-thirds of American women have had an abortion, compared with less than one-third in Britain. About 40% of births in the United States are unplanned – double the British proportion.

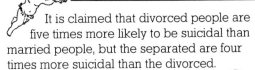

It is claimed that divorced people are five times more likely to be suicidal than married people, but the separated are four times more suicidal than the divorced.

Nevada, long famous as a venue for 'quickie' divorces, has always kept its residential qualifying period the shortest in the USA: divorce was one of the state's major industries.

In 1931, the American State of Nevada 'created' two major industries – gambling and divorce. Reno and Las Vegas were for many years famous as the nation's divorce capitals, largely because Nevada's divorce laws were so liberal. Eventually, however, the laws of many other states relaxed and the two towns lost their notoriety, though Nevada remained the gambling and entertainment capital of the US.

most frequently cite their wives' adultery as the cause of marriage breakdown. The fifth condition, desertion, is rarely cited by either.

At present in a contested divorce case, one partner is obliged to prove that, at least, the other has behaved unreasonably. There is – as yet – no such thing as a 'no default' divorce in Britain.

Before the **1857 Matrimonial Causes Act**, judicial separation (ie divorce) could only be granted by ecclesiastical courts, and even then remarriage was prohibited except where an applicant was rich enough to have a special private bill passed in Parliament.

In 1971, the **Divorce Reform Act 1969** came into force in England and Wales and the number of decrees made absolute during that year was less than half the number in 1988. Seventy-two per cent of all decrees granted in England and Wales in 1988 were to wives.

On 12th October, 1984, Section 1 of the **Matrimonial and Family Proceeds Act 1984** became law. It allowed couples to petition for divorce after the first anniversary of their marriage; previously they'd had to wait until at least the third anniversary. This led to a 6% increase in divorce petitions in 1985, with a record 191 000 in England and Wales that year.

Glyn 'Scotty' De Moss Wolff (born in 1908) of Blythe, California, was at one time a Baptist minister. He has married 27 wives monogamously, the first in 1927. When he married his 18th bride, Ester Katz (aged 18), at Las Vegas in 1967, they drove off in opposite directions after the ceremony. His latest wife, Daisy Delgado, is 62 years younger than he is. He thinks he has about 40 children.

The longest divorce trial in the UK took place in 1962. It lasted 28 days, after which Alfred George Boyd Gibbons was granted a decree nisi against his wife Dorothy for her adultery with John Halperin of New York City.

Linda Lou Essex of Anderson, Indiana, has been through 21 monogamous marriages to 15 different men – the first wedding was in 1957 and the most recent divorce was in 1988.

Barmaid Beverley Nina Avery of Los Angeles, California, had been through 16 divorces by 1957, when she was 48 years old. Fourteen husbands were involved, five of whom, she alleged, had broken her nose.

St Uncumber was the name Sir Thomas More gave to the Portuguese saint, Wilgefortis (who grew a beard to discourage her suitors). She was said to 'uncumber' women of unwanted husbands for a peck of oats.

In Sir Thomas More's *Utopia* divorce was allowed either by mutual consent or for adultery or 'intolerable waywardness', and the guilty party was not permitted to remarry. 'Breakers of wedlock' were punished by bondage. Sir Thomas (1478–1535) was married twice. He met his end when he was beheaded for refusing to acknowledge King Henry VIII as head of the Church of England, and he was canonised in 1935.

Farmers have unique problems. Perhaps the most common and literally down-to-earth example of business and marriage being well and truly bound together is on the farm, where very often the wife is as essential to the business as the husband, either because she works on the farm itself, or because she gives her husband the vital domestic support he needs. In addition, of course, the home is part of the business. For many couples whose marriages are under stress in rural conditions (which often means isolation) and with the increasing depression in agriculture, the financial and social implications of separating seem even more terrible than enduring an impossible marriage.

As Tessa Gates wrote in *Farmer's Weekly*: 'A farm marriage is different . . . When you marry a farmer, you not only take on a husband but a business, and possibly a whole set of relatives who are also business partners.' It is farming, as a business, that is likely to ruin a farming marriage, rather than extramarital affairs for which both partners are probably too tired anyway!

In 1987, Dr Bridget Hester of the National Marriage Guidance Council (now known as Relate), completed a two-year study of the relationships of 95 people in north east England and concluded that children whose warring parents stayed together 'for the sake of the children' were more likely to end up in unsuccessful marriages themselves than those whose parents divorced or separated. The findings suggest that children are able to sense unhappy atmospheres, however much the parents pretend that all is well. It seems that children brought up in such tense households grow up to choose their partners from similar backgrounds and, as both are less able to cope with marriage because of those backgrounds – the chances of disaster are doubled!

By 1985, 13% of families in the UK had only one parent. By 1989–90 there were about 600 000 single-parent families headed by the mother and 80 000 headed by the father, in cases of divorce or separation (the figures did not take widowed parents into account).

The **divorce rate** in England and Wales is almost the highest in Europe – four out of every 10 marriages end in divorce and there are 160 000 divorces a year. One in seven of the marriages involved have broken up before the fifth wedding anniversary. The highest overall divorce rate in the UK is among those who have been married for five to nine years but not surprisingly, once they have made it to the silver wedding anniversary, the rate drops considerably. The rate is highest among teenage marriages – about half of them end in divorce.

From 1981 to 1987, the rate of divorce in the European Community had increased for all countries except the Netherlands (excluding the Republic of Ireland, where it is illegal). Denmark had the highest rate in 1987, at 12.1 for every 1000 existing marriages that year, compared with the UK's 11.9. In Italy the rate was far lower at only 0.9 per 1000.

Nearly a quarter of all the divorces in England and Wales in 1988 involved at least one partner who had been divorced before. It seems that we never learn!

The American divorce rate is the highest in the world. In 1987, there were 1.157 million divorces in the USA. It was estimated that 2% of all existing marriages had broken up during 1986. In 1900, there had been only 55 751 divorces, a rate of 0.7 per 1000 population, but the rate had more than doubled by 1920 to 1.6 (170 505). It reached a peak of 4.3 (610 000) in 1946 – the same year for the peak marriage rate – but dropped back to less than 3 per 1000 population for the next two decades. The number of US divorces hit the million mark in 1975.

As with marriage, each American state has its own laws on divorce. In all of them, it is necessary for one or both parties to reside in the state for a statutory period before a divorce can be considered, and the waiting time varies from South Dakota's 'physical presence plus intent to make the state a place of residence' and Alaska's 'no residency requirement but action will not be heard by court until 30 days after filing for divorce', to a whole year's residence in a dozen states and two years in Rhode Island. Nevada remains one of the least demanding states, with a six-week residential requirement, and most states now place no restriction period before a divorcee can remarry.

Acceptable **grounds for divorce** in the US vary from state to state, but most states accept:

Adultery	Pregnancy at marriage
Cruelty	(husband not knowing)
Desertion	Bigamy
Alcoholism	Separation
Impotence	Indignities
Conviction for felony	Drug addiction
Neglect to provide	Violence
Insanity	Fraudulent contract

In addition, there are all sorts of other grounds which are acceptable in the various states, including:

Incompatibility
Irretrievable breakdown of marital relationship
Relationship within prohibited degree
Infamous crime
Crime against nature
Excessively vicious conduct
Conduct detrimental to marriage relationship
Attempt by one party on life of other
Wickedness
Physical cruelty
Violation of conjugal duty
Treatment such as to injure health or endanger reason
Gross neglect of duty
Habitual intemperance
Infected other party with communicable venereal disease
Joined a religious cult disbelieving in marriage
Public defamation
Wife's refusal to remove with husband to another state
Wife wilfully absenting herself for two years
Abuse of a child
Voluntary non-cohabitation
Abandonment

And , in Washington DC, you can actually have a 'no-default' divorce.

Back in the Dark Ages (5th–8th centuries), kings felt that only the Church could solemnise a marriage. However, they feared that if the Church declared a marriage invalid there could be a dynastic war. The Church thus found itself in a strong position to oppose royal divorces – that is, until Henry VIII came along. The declaration that his marriage to Catharine of Aragon was invalid and his marriage to Anne Boleyn, in 1533, precipitated the **Act of Supremacy** whereby Henry VIII became supreme head of the Church of England.

Confucius, the Chinese philosopher (c 550–478 BC), cited seven 'good' reasons for divorcing a woman:

She is rebellious towards her in-laws
She fails to produce a son
She is unfaithful
She is jealous of her husband's other women
She has an incurable or repulsive disease
She has a spiteful tongue and is a gossip
She is a thief

The Latin word *nisi* means 'unless' and is used in the legal context to describe a decision which should take effect unless, after a time, some specified condition is fulfilled. In the case of divorce, a decree nisi is one that becomes absolute unless cause is shown to the contrary. The word 'divorce' is from the same root as 'divert', in the sense of turning away from someone.

In February, 1984, in Milwaukee, a divorce was granted to Simon Stern, aged 96, and his wife Ida, 91. This is the current world record for the oldest divorcees.

In November, 1980, Harry Bidwell was divorced at Brighton, in Sussex. He was 101 years old.

In the 9th century, the Frankish King Lothair II of Lorraine demanded a divorce. His kingdom's bishops complied but were promptly deposed by Pope Nicholas I (858–867), who refused the king's plea.

Among the **Ashanti** tribe of West Africa, if a couple are divorced, the sons are likely to remain with the father and the daughters with the mother. In the earlier days, even during the marriage, the sons would move at puberty into their mother's brother's household and the uncle was responsible for the cost of their education rather than the father. (It was originally a society of matrilineal inheritance.)

In Nepal, a **Nedwar** woman can divorce her husband by simply placing a betel nut under his pillow.

MONEY MATTERS

Alimony is an allowance made by a man (usually) to a woman during or after their divorce or legal separation. The word is derived from the Latin *alere*, to nourish. **Palimony** is an American term coined to describe 'divorce' settlements for unmarried couples.

The then very rich couple, Donald and Ivana Trump, liked to promote themselves as the perfect pair. They were also business partners, which both sealed and soured their marital relationship. After a much publicised affair of Donald's, the couple were pictured publicly holding hands at an Easter family outing, reconciled by what was termed a 'carnal contract' by which, it seems, Ivana accepted that adultery was part of American marriage, so long as *both* partners could indulge in it. The contract was limited to 60 days, after which it could be renewed. However, the couple became divorced on 11th December, 1990. The presiding judge said that Donald's 'cruel and inhuman' treatment of Ivana 'made it improper to continue to be married'.

British actress Jenny Seagrove's highly publicised divorce from Madhav Sharma took three years to settle and the final traumatic stages included a tug-of-love for a 10-year-old brown and white spaniel called Tasha. As a puppy, Tasha was given by Jenny to her mother, but soon became Jenny's own pet and went with her when she married Sharma. In 1986, the couple separated, but the following year Jenny left the dog with her estranged husband while she was filming in Israel. During the bitter divorce proceedings which followed, she discovered that the dog was deemed to be a chattel of the marriage, and its ownership could not be settled until the final hearing on financial matters – unless mutual agreement could be reached beforehand.

Ten thousand pounds later Jenny regained ownership of Tasha and in February, 1990, a publican from Suffolk brought the dog to the BBC Television Centre's car park in west London at 11pm, where the assembled cast included a senior divorce solicitor, an articled clerk from another law firm, and Madhav Sharma. By the cold neon car park lights, Tasha was ceremoniously transferred into a car with the publican and two of Jenny's legal representatives, while the articled clerk and Sharma climbed into a second vehicle. The convoy then proceeded to Farnham, Surrey, where Sharma bade farewell to the bemused Tasha and the dog was returned to the tender care of Jenny's mother.

The overall cost of ending the couple's childless two-year marriage came to £250 000. It involved five firms of solicitors, four Queen's Counsels and six junior counsels and it took three years and 20 court appearances before judges and registrars. It left one side dogless and both sides penniless. Moral: are you quite sure that you want to marry?

American **Marvin Mitchelson** is well known as an alimony and palimony lawyer. In 1983, he successfully obtained an award of $81 million for his client, Belgian-born Sheika Dena Al-Fassi, aged 23. She had actually filed for $3000 million in Los Angeles a year earlier against her husband Mohammed Al-Fassi, aged 28, a member of the Saudi Arabian royal family. During the case, Mitchelson pointed out that the Sheikh had 14 homes in Florida alone.

Raoul Felder, an American matrimonial lawyer, says that, on divorce, a woman should expect to get the equivalent of a rich husband's annual

Robert Carrol of Ashland, Wisconsin, is a lorry driver. His wife entered into an adulterous relationship with another (unemployed) lorry driver brought in as a lodger by Robert as a friendly gesture to a mate in trouble. After a bitter divorce, he pressed adultery charges against his wife knowing full well that, according to Wisconsin law, she faced the possibility of a fine of $10 000 (£6000) and two years' imprisonment if found guilty. Who said that hell hath no fury like a *woman* scorned?!

Mrs Anne Bass is reputed to have rejected a settlement of $535 million from her ex-husband Sid, in Texas, because she deemed it 'inadequate' to live on in the style to which she had become accustomed.

Although £5000 was considered the record alimony awarded in a British court in the 1960s, the 2nd Duke of Westmister (1879–1953) had made a settlement of £13 000 per annum to his first wife, Constance Edwina (née Cornwallis-West) in 1919.

income, plus an annuity sum of about 10% of that income. In some states (California, for example) the wife is entitled to half her husband's total wealth, or to at least half of the wealth acquired during the marriage.

America's richest man, **John Kluge** (born in 1914), recently separated from his British-born wife, former bellydancer and nude model Patricia Rose Gay, aged 41. She expects a settlement of £650 million, which would make her the richest woman in America. Her husband, who considered her his 'greatest treasure', had carelessly failed to draw up a pre-nuptial contract before their marriage in 1981. Such a settlement would easily beat the record £500 million for **Soraya Kashoggi**, who also received property from her ex-husband Adnan.

WIFE FOR SALE!

The selling of a wife was an informal method of divorce which continued well into the 19th century (by which time her price had become a pint of beer). People sincerely believed that the practice was legal as long as the following traditional conditions were met:

The deal was made in public
The wife consented, at least in theory
The wife was brought to the place of sale wearing a straw halter round her neck to validate the sale
She was not sold for less than a shilling

Thomas Hardy's novel *The Mayor of Casterbridge* was published in 1886 and contains a classic description of the sale of a wife to a sailor for five guineas. In this case, however, the husband Michael, an out-of-work hay-trusser, was decidedly drunk at the time and had put his wife, Susan, up for sale as a joke, offering her "to any man that will pay me the money, and treat her well; and he shall have her for ever, and never hear aught o' me." It took him many years and many heartaches to find her again – and thereby hangs a tale.

When sold to the highest bidder, she became the purchaser's wife and the original husband felt free to remarry, believing that the woman had no further claim on him. In fact, it has never been permissible in English law to sell wives.

A man called John Lees sold his wife for sixpence in 1796.

A Lancashire man sold his wife in 1831 for three shillings and sixpence and a gallon of ale. Then he persuaded the town crier to ring his bell and tell the world that he was no longer responsible for her future debts.

In Carlisle, Cumbria, in 1832, a man called Joseph Thomson sold his wife Mary Anne to

An 1844 illustration of the horrific former Hindu custom of suttee whereby a widow threw herself on her late husband's funeral pyre.

Henry Mears for 20 shillings (£1) and a New-foundland dog. In spite of his having advertised her as a tormentor and a domestic curse, they parted amicably.

In 1858, a Yorkshireman sold his pretty young wife at a beer shop at Little Horton, simply because they did not get on with each other. Rather sweetly, he led her to the place of sale with a rib-bon round her neck rather than a straw halter or a rope.

In 1881, a woman in a London court produced a stamped receipt to prove that she had been sold for 25 shillings some years before and was there-fore 'lawfully' wed to her second husband.

In Blackwood, Monmouthshire, in 1928, a man told a magistrate's court that he had sold his wife for £1 and had a document from the purchaser to prove it. He kept the child from the marriage as it was his own flesh and blood.

WIDOWED

The word 'widow' comes from the Latin *vidua* meaning a woman bereft of her husband.

In many cultures, widows are well cared for by their husbands' relatives.

On the death of a **Riffian** husband (the Riffians are peoples in North Africa), his brother takes on his widow and children in a form of economic and social polygyny.

Among several of the **Indian** tribes on the northwest coast of the American continent, a man's property passes to his sister's son when he dies. Boys live with their maternal uncle from the age of six to eight and, when the uncle dies, his nephew often marries his aged widow, assuming the uncle's name and taking his property. In Africa, too, the widow of a man of the **Gwambe** tribe is inherited by her late husband's nephew.

Roses are the traditional flowers of love. Red

rose bushes are often planted at the head of a sweetheart's grave, and many are the stories of wild roses springing up spontaneously at the graves of faithful lovers and reaching out to entwine each other.

In **Wales** a red rose used to be planted on the grave of someone particularly kind and good, while a white rose was planted on a virgin's grave.

In **Sweden**, married women wore their hair braided and were buried thus when they died, in contrast to young girls, who wore their hair loose and were buried with a mirror when they died, so that they could tidy their hair on Judgement Day!

The 'hairy **Ainu**' people of Hokkaido, Japan, are so proud of their hairiness that women even tattoo moustaches on their upper lips! A widow, however, cuts her hair short.

In the **Andaman Islands**, in the Bay of Bengal, it used to be the custom for a widow to wear her late husband's skull, hanging in front of her from a necklace.

Kingfishers, outwardly such gorgeous, jewel-coloured birds that dart like a flash of light across the water, are said to be reincarnations of the souls of faithful couples united in death. The basis of this belief stems from the Greek legend of **Halcyone**, wife of the King of Trachis. The king drowned at sea after a shipwreck and she, unaware of the tragedy, waited patiently for his return until his fate was revealed to her in a dream. Devastated, she plunged into the sea, but the gods changed the devoted couple into kingfishers so that they could again live happily and faithfully together by the water.

The shortest valid will in the world is 'Vse zene', which is Czech for 'All to my wife' and was written on 19th January, 1967, by Herr Karl Tausch of Langen, Hesse, in Germany.

There was a three-word will stating 'All for Mother' in England in 1906 – it was originally contested in the case of Thorn vs Dickens but was subsequently admitted to probate in English law.

The Ancient Greeks thought that kingfishers floated their nests on the sea and that the gods decreed that the birds should always be granted a period of calm weather while the eggs were being incubated. This belief, combined with the legend, gave rise to the term 'halcyon days' (meaning a period of peace and happiness) for the seven days before, and seven days after, the winter solstice, when the birds were said to be brooding and there were no storms at sea. In France, the kingfisher is linked with St Martin's feast day on 11th November, when there is often a period of fine weather known as St Martin's Summer.

HAPPILY EVER AFTER

In spite of the adversities, much cynicism and the rising divorce rates, many couples do indeed live happily together ever after, or at least remain content with each other's company.

Amelia was the model of wifely affection who gave her name to the title of Henry Fielding's last novel (published in 1751). The main character was based on his own wife, who was described in William Thackeray's *Vanity Fair* as 'one of the best and dearest creatures'.

Adam Borntrager of Medford, Wisconsin, died in 1984 at the age of 96 when he had 707 direct descendants (all but 32 living): 11 children, 115 grandchildren, 529 great-grandchildren and 20 great-great-grandchildren. Mrs Peter L Schwartz (1902–88) had 14 children, 175 grandchildren, 477 great-grandchildren and 20 great-great-grandchildren. Imagine remembering all the birthdays! Both these prolific people were Amish Mennonites – a sect which firmly rejects 20th-century 'progress'.

The affectionate term 'my old dutch' has nothing to do with the Netherlands. It is a Cockney slang expression for 'duchess'.

The most beautiful, romantic and magnificent memorial to a beloved wife must be the Taj Mahal, built by Shah Jahan (1628–1658) in tribute to his queen, Mumtaz Mahal, who was buried in its huge white-marble mausoleum. She died in 1631 and it took 20 years for 20 000 workers to build her tomb and shrine. The marble was transported from Rajasthan's Makrana mines and the immense dome, 246ft (75m) high and weighing about 12 000 tonnes, was originally sheathed in gold while from Arabia, China and Europe came the thousands of semi-precious stones (including agate, onyx, lapis lazuli, chalcedony and crystal) used as decorative inlay. The Taj Mahal, reflected in the moonlit water of its garden, is indescribably lovely and, despite its grandeur, a delicate and moving declaration of marital love.

The Taj Mahal, loving tribute to an adored wife.

Jack V Moran of Seattle, USA, and his wife Edna married in July, 1937, at Seaside, Oregon, and clearly enjoyed the occasion. Since then they have married each other again – and again and again, indeed 40 times in many different venues including London and Cairo.

The longest recorded marriages both lasted for 86 years. Cousins **Sir Temulji Bhicaji Nariman** and **Lady Nariman** married in 1853 when both were five years old and the marriage lasted until his death in Bombay in 1940, when he was nearly 92. **Lazarus Rowe** of Greenland, New Hampshire, USA, married **Mary Webber** in 1743. He died before her in 1829.

The British record is held by **James Frederick Burgess** (born 1861) and **Sarah Ann**, née Gregory (born 1865). They married in London, in 1883, and their marriage lasted 82 years – they died within months of each other.

The most golden weddings in one family is ten. The **Gresi** family is headed by Joseph and Sophia Gresi of Manitowoc, Wisconsin, and their six sons and four daughters all celebrated golden wedding anniversaries between April, 1962 and September, 1988. The family of **George** and **Eleanor Hopkins** of Patrick County, Virginia, claim a similar record for the period between November, 1961 and October, 1988.

In Britain, **Mr** and **Mrs J Stredwick** of East Sussex had three sons and four daughters who all celebrated their golden weddings between May, 1971 and April, 1981.

The 'Dunmow Flitch' is a side of bacon awarded in a custom instituted in the year 1111 by Juga, a noblewoman, and restored in 1244 by Robert de Fitzwalter. It is given to any person who claims it by going to Dunmow (in Essex) and kneeling on two sharp stones at the church door, as long as he can solemnly swear that, for 12 months and a day, he has never once had a household argument, or wished himself unmarried. Between 1244 and 1772, only seven claimants were awarded the Flitch:

1445: Richard Wright, labourer, Bawburgh, near Norwich
1467: Steven Samuel, occupation unknown, Little Ayston, Essex
1510: Thomas Ley, fuller, Coggeshall, Essex
1701: William Parsley, butcher, Much-Easton, Essex (it was also awarded to his wife, Jane)
1751: Thomas Shakeshaft, woolcomber, Weathersfield, Essex
1763: Awarded, but name not recorded
1773: John and Susan Gilder, occupation unknown, Tarling, Essex

The custom was revived in the 19th century, and in 1854 W Harrison Ainsworth wrote *The Flitch of Bacon or The Custom of Dunmow*, dedicating it to Baron and Baroness Tauchnitz. The dedication read: "As a record of rare conjugal attachment, this Tale may be appropriately inscribed to you, my good friends: than whom I have never known a more fondly-united couple."

HAPPY ANNIVERSARY

1st:	Cotton
2nd:	Paper
3rd:	Leather
4th:	Flowers or fruit
5th:	Wood
6th:	Iron
7th:	Wool
8th:	Bronze
9th:	Copper or pottery
10th:	Tin
11th:	Steel
12th:	Silk and fine linen
13th:	Lace
14th:	Ivory
15th:	Crystal
20th:	China
25th:	Silver
30th:	Pearl
35th:	Coral
40th:	Ruby
45th:	Sapphire
50th:	Gold
55th:	Emerald
60th:	Diamond
70th:	Platinum

Bibliography

Alexander, Marc, *British Folklore, Myths and Legends*, Weidenfeld & Nicolson, 1982

Baker, Margaret, *Wedding Customs and Folklore*, David & Charles, 1977

Bold, Alan ed, *The Picador Book of Erotic Verse*, Picador, 1983

Bulfinch, Thomas, *Bulfinch's Complete Mythology*, Spring Books, 1989

Cosby, Bill, *Love and Marriage*, Guild Publishing, 1989

Derraugh, Patricia and William, *Wedding Etiquette For All Denominations*, W. Foulsham & Co., 1971

Fromm, Erich, *The Art of Loving*, Unwin Hyman

Garlick, Helen and Stuart Sheppard, Jane, *The Good Marriage*, Simon & Schuster, 1990

Halley, Ned ed, *All You Need is Love: A Dateline Guide to Life and Love in the 90s*, Sphere Books, 1990

Heaton, Vernon, *The Best Man's Duties*, Elliot Right Way Books, 1967

Hite, Shere, *Women and Love: A Cultural Revolution in Progress*, Viking

Jeffery, Barbara, *Wedding Speeches and Toasts*, W. Foulsham & Co., 1971

Kent, Margaret, *How to Marry the Man of Your Choice*, Robson Books, 1988

Lansdell, Avril, *Wedding Fashions 1860–1980*, Shire Publications

Lau, Theodora, *The Handbook of Chinese Horoscopes*, Souvenir Press, 1979

Lawrence, Margaret, *Wedding Etiquette*, Ward Lock, 1963

Nown, Graham ed, *Coronation Street 1960–1985*, Ward Lock, 1985

Prickett, John ed, *Marriage and the Family*, Lutterworth Press *Living Faith* series, 1985

Radford, E. and M.A., *Encyclopaedia of Superstitions*, Hutchinson, 3rd edition 1969

Rees, Alwyn and Brinley, *Celtic Heritage: Ancient Tradition in Ireland and Wales*, Thames & Hudson, 1978

Rubinstein, Helge ed, *The Oxford Book of Marriage*, Oxford University Press, 1990

Shuel, Brian, *Guide to the Traditional Customs of Britain*, Webb & Bower and Michael Joseph, 1985

Young, Lailan, *Love Around the World*, Hodder & Stoughton, 1985

Index

INDEX OF QUOTATIONS